Hit Me With Your Best Shot!

Hit Me With Your Best Shot!

How I Overcame A Hard-Hitting Life

<Self-published/ Neena Perez >
<2019>

For more information:
hello@straighttalknosugaradded.com

FIRST PRINTING 2018
ISBN-13: 978-1727778045

www.straighttalknosugaradded.com
Hello@straighttalknosugaradded.com

You may purchase on:
Amazon.com
Kindle
Lulu.com
Ingramspark.com

Forward by:
Kelly Balarie, 10/2018
Author, National Speaker, Blogger at
www.purposefulfaith.com

Photography done by:
Christine Simmons portraiture
P.O. box 1706
New Canaan, CT 06840
christine@christinesimmons.com
www.christinesimmons.com

Dedication

**To my God, my husband Rudy, my boys Ernest and Justin
and my bonus children Christian and Stephanie.
My life would not be worth writing if it wasn't for God and
you all in it!!**

Acknowledgements

First to My God
I want to acknowledge you First because I spent most of my life not acknowledging you and not realizing how much you were there for me even when I didn't know you. I love you Lord and Thank you for snatching me out of the mess and showing me beauty. Life hit me hard but you help me hit it back!

My family
I want to dedicate this to my amazing family. My beautiful husband, Rudy, who has been there for me through thick and thin. No one else in the world I would've chosen to do this with. Thank you for always being supportive even when I do crazy things. You are such an amazing, authentic, loving, true, faithful, encouraging man, and I hope that one day, I could be half as amazing to you as you are to me.

My firstborn baby boy, Ernest. You were sent by God to save my life when I didn't think I wanted it anymore. You are so special to me, and besides God, you will forever be my first true love.

My second born, Justin, the one God made sure was born on purpose and for a purpose despite all the obstacles. You are a warrior and a true gift from Heaven above! The love I have for you cannot be measured.

Christian and Stephanie, my life would not be complete without you both. I can't believe how lucky I am to be so blessed with two extra amazing kids from God. Thank you for letting me be in your lives and allowing me to love you with all my heart! I am truly blessed.

Extended family.

To my mom who gave birth to me when she was scared. I love you, mom. Despite all we have gone through, I'm grateful you are my mother. God bless you, mom. Bendición.

My Grandparents, who took the role of my parents and loved me so very much. I can't wait until we see each other again. Thank you for all the lessons in my life. I love you so much!

To my aunts and uncles, you all played a part in molding me. I loved watching you all and taking for myself the parts I loved the most like having good friends, being hardworking, educated and tough.

To my awesome cousins who were always willing to support me when I felt unsupported. You know who you are and how you came into my life when I needed you the most!

And of course, my cousin, Maria, who was there to open the door to my family and me on more than one occasion. I love you so very much, you are not my cousin but my sister.

My brothers, Edgar and Frankie, my sister, Maydaliz who helped me get out of the darkness because they were born. I will never be able to express how much you all mean to me. Thank you for all my beautiful nieces and nephews.

My brothers, sisters, nieces and nephews from my biological dad. I'm so glad we found each other. It has meant so much to me to be a part of Dad's kids even though I didn't have too much of an opportunity to be with him. You all accepted and loved me anyway, and I can't express to you how much I needed that!

Friends

Marybell, who has saved my life more than anyone should. You have always been there to help, protect, love, and sometimes, carry me. You will always be more than a friend. Thirty years of friendship and counting into eternity.

Lucy, my spiritual leader, sister, and friend. You are my door opener in more ways than one. The one who gave us somewhere to lay our heads when we didn't have even a shoulder to lean on. Thank you for always keeping it real with me and not sugarcoating anything. My root.

My sisters and brothers in Christ. You know who you are. Many of you have been such an intricate part of my growth. From encouragers, spiritual leaders, choir directors, church members, pastors, and friends. God bless you and the work of your hands abundantly. Thank you for being my adopted family.

Forward

Healing can come from a variety of places.

I've found healing after hearing the simple sound of my son's laughter. Suddenly, I remember, I can be a child too. And, I've found healing after a quiet hike through the woods. Here, I remember, the world is bigger than me and it is orchestrated by someone far more knowledgeable than me. I've found healing after looking to others for answers. After doing that, I've come to realize we're all on our own search and everyone is – in process. But, one of the most profound ways, I've found healing is through stories. I don't think I'm alone.

It is why we love Super Bowl ads. It is why we migrate towards television. It is why testimonies of hardship, endurance and breakthrough capture us. It is why in biblical times Jesus told dozens of parables.

When someone puts a finger on the exact pain you've had a hard time voicing, it brings healing. When someone describes what they were thinking, feeling or enduring, you remember that you are not alone. When someone travels through hell and back, even if their story doesn't look exactly like yours, you gain courage to endure and press on. You feel seen. You feel understood. You feel thankful that they made it. You feel thankful that you can make it too.

You learn from their hardship. You glean wisdom from their understanding of difficulty. You understand that pain is universal and so is complete victory, if you get the opportunity to know Jesus.

Neena's story captures me this way. It is not that I've endured everything she has. This is not the point, nor the breakthrough. Her details don't have to be my details. Never measure your trials or testimony against someone else's. The point is not what they've gone through or what you've gone through; the point is who you've become. Who you are today. And, who Neena's become inspires me more than anything. Even though, what she has gone through is most certainly riveting, heart-wrenching and put-your-hand-over-your mouth terrifying. Even though, by worldly accounts some would say she's "earned her stripes", astonishingly, this is not her badge of honor.

Her badge of honor is the force that never let her quit. It is the miraculous internal sense, or calling, nearly nudging at her to say, "Neena, you are made for more." It is the pull of love. It is the Holy Spirit in her, that always demolishes defeat and establishes victory.

This is Neena's strength to overcome; it can be yours too. Let her words inspire you. Let them lead you to greater love. Let them deliver you into the hands of complete healing. So much so that you no longer need to partner with terror, horror, fear, disappointment, discouragement, defeat or demoralization any longer.

"Hit Me with Your Best Shot" is not only Neena's story, but it's your story too. Look the glimmers of life that are speaking to you. See the way of escape in your life - the doorway to your own personal healing. Go after it. Allow Neena's words to draw out yours.

Allow her sentences to define new sentences of prayers. Allow her voice to give voice to the one you've silenced. Allow her wisdom to strengthen you. Allow her fight-back strategy to give you a resilient warrior-like spirit that won't back down. Allow her stampede over shame to annihilate yours.

You don't have to believe anymore that you're destined to live a life where you *always get hit.* You don't have to lay down like a doormat any longer. You don't have to exist - fearing the shoe is going to drop, yet again.

Let the victory of God displayed in Neena's life, become yours too. If you feel like you can't, or don't know how, ask Jesus. Ask Him, "How, God? Show me the way." God's never led anyone wrong. He's never turned, abandoned a single person who wants His help. Nor has He ever turned away from those calling out in need.

Neena's life is proof-point and a test-case of this. It is a glory-story. It is a get on your boxing gloves, put on your armor and step-out-into-battle, I-ain't-going-down-easy, I-am-going-to-believe-no-matter-what story that will catapult your inner strength and courage to new levels.

What is coming against you is not your demise, it is your up rise. What meant to take you down, will do none of that, rather, it will lift you higher into God's love. What intended to harm you, will instead be nullified and God will, instead, prosper you with a hope and a future.

May your heart find new trust. May you discover your personal victory. May resiliency hit you afresh. May you realize how loved you really are. May you know – no matter how bad things look, goodness is always above you and no hit is ever too strong for God's power that fights back.

You are safe. Loved. Adored. Secure. Called. Helped. And resilient. Just like Neena. May all this surface as you turn every page, read every sentence and wipe away every tear. Get ready for a profound journey as you travel through Neena's story.

Kelly Balarie, 10/2018
Author of "Battle Ready Train your Mind to Conquer Challenges, Defeat Doubt and Live Victoriously" and "Fear Fighting: Awakening Courage to Overcome Your Fears", National Speaker, Blogger at www.purposefulfaith.com

Introduction

My goal in writing this book is to share with you a bit of all I've been through in life, in the hopes that I can connect with you even in a small way. We all have our stories, we all have something that connects us in some way, whether it's large or small, either it's funny, sad, tragic, or just plain dumb.

This book has been in the making for forty-five years. When I was about twenty-one years old, I remember writing what I thought was a blockbuster hit of my real-life story. I got to about four chapters in my mega book deal of the future. I don't know if you remember floppy disks, but I used to have an electric typewriter that used floppy disks and that's where I started writing my book. Of course, I lost my floppy disk because I loaned the typewriter to someone and never got the floppy disk back. So, it's been another twenty-five years or so since that happened and being that this is my first book, you can guess that my so-called blockbuster hit never really happened. I'm glad! Because the following twenty-five years just added to the colors and richness, pain and growth, that I've experienced in my life. I do pray that this book shows you a little bit of me or a lot of me since the book is about me. My prayer is that you will laugh a little, cry a little, see yourself maybe a little bit in this book, get frustrated a little, but also see how to overcome, to win, to not give up, to cry, to stand when you feel like falling and to realize that you will be bent in life, but you will not be broken!

This book is not about God entirely, it is about my life before I knew God, when I was getting to know God, and now that I know God! I will never hide who I am; I am not ashamed of it. I feel like it is all of the hard things that I have been through in my life that make me who I am today. I have been a mess, have caused messes in my life. It has been very challenging, but there has been beauty in a mess. We do things in our life we can't control, a lot of things in our life we can control but choose not to, and a lot of things in our life we invite in. I don't know about you, but a lot of times, I feel like a hot mess! I don't always feel pretty, I don't always feel strong, I don't always feel smart, I don't always feel loved, but what I do feel, however, is that I will make it through another day if God is willing. I've learned throughout the years that even though we are not promised tomorrow, we shouldn't let today destroy us.

I'll try to take you through my life from the beginning and up to or close to where I am now. Some stories, especially in the beginning, were stories that were told to me by my close relatives because I have a very light to no memory before five years old. But even before four or five years of age, there were quite a few things that happened to me, and I think it's because of that trauma that I can't remember. There are holes that I can't seem to fill. It can get frustrating sometimes when you're trying to put a puzzle together and when you look at the puzzle, there are holes in it. At times, it just doesn't feel complete! So, I will do my best to share with you the truth of those years according to the witnesses my family gave me where my memory fails. It's funny how the body does that, isn't it? The way your brain shut things out that are going to hurt you.

For many years now, friends and family have been persuading me to write a book! Write a book—are they crazy? Who wants to sit and read my life story? I wouldn't want to depress anyone. If you know me, and hopefully if you don't, you'll get to know some of me in this book. You will know that I am not the gushiest, mushy, sensitive type of person, but I'll tell it like it is, truly with the best intentions at heart.

Even right now, as I write all these words on paper, I thought, *Neena, are you good enough? Is anybody even interested in your story? Why are you so important anyway? When you bring this out and you tell your truth, will your family talk to you? Will your mom talk to you? Will your children even read this book? What are you leaving behind, anything good?* I decided to write it anyway because I am stubborn!

I have spent way too many years doubting, fighting, beating myself up, getting beat up, being put down, and feeling defeated! Even if I'm the only one that reads this book, I'm doing it! So, here it goes. I'm about to do probably one of the hardest things I have done to date—tell my story from my perspective of hurts, pain, depression, anxiety, anger and also of love, overcoming, strength, and faith.

Forgive me if what you're looking for is the book with lots of "Christianese," I'm afraid you will not find that here. You may, however, find a bit of cursing, sarcasm, confusion, frustration, sadness, happiness, blessings and other emotions I can't think of.

I'm just a woman that has been through much in life, learned a few lessons along the way, and have much more to learn…

Thank you! Yes, you! Thank you for picking up this book and giving me a look over; I am eternally grateful!

Chapter 1

IN THE BEGINNING

I remember opening up my eyes and lying in the bed that had sheets that were yellow with little flowers on them. I looked up and saw a very bright light passing through the window, and I said in my mind, I am here, I made it. That was the day that my mother brought me home from the hospital and laid me down in her little room—on her bed. Don't ask me how I remember that moment; I was merely just a few days old, but I do remember that moment, and then I don't remember much of anything up until the age of four or five. I thought this was just a dream or a figment of my imagination, but I couldn't shake it. So, one day, I decided as crazy as it sounds that I was going to ask my mother. She verified that those were the sheets in the room I was describing, and she had absolutely no idea how I would know that. We just looked at each other for a few seconds, trying to understand how that's possible. She couldn't fathom it and neither could I. I can only recant to you the stories that I've heard of the things that have occurred to me from that day until the age of five.

I'll start by saying that I've always considered myself the *oops baby*. I was conceived by accident. My mother was married, and my father was married—just not to each other. My mom was a beautiful, sexy young lady of about 20 years old and my father was a very handsome man with hazel eyes as you gaze at them. I can imagine her just looking at him and being completely enveloped in his handsome, beautiful, wavy hair and his eyes that sucked you into the darkness of who he was.

My mom was married to a man that was an alcoholic and abusive, cruel and barely attentive to the fact that he had such an amazingly beautiful wife. Whenever I bring up the subject or tried to ask her, she does not like to admit nor talk about that entire situation, I can just imagine that the arms of a handsome, smooth-talking, charismatic man were just what she needed to escape a horrible marriage which felt more like a prison but was her reality. I hear the stories from family relatives about my mom being in fear because she was pregnant and she knew it did not belong to her husband. You can imagine she must've been so frightened. What does she do now!? I mean she's Catholic, so there is no way an abortion is going to happen. But this is also the type of sin that is exposed monthly as the belly grows and the time draws nigh when you can no longer hide a human being that has been formed in the womb.

Well, there is my father; he was as irresponsible as he was handsome. He knew I was his, he knew I was coming but didn't know how to tell his wife or even expose it! He decided not to. I really wasn't worth breaking up a marriage where he had a child already. He just had a baby that was turning 11 months old when I was born. His wife did find out and gave him an ultimatum, it's either their family or me? He chose them, walked away, never gave me his name, never cared for me. In other words, I was rejected from birth. I could imagine how that must've hurt my mother deeply and maybe even caused her to look at me with a little bit of resentment that I would bring all this calamity and pain.

What do you do when you are miserable in a marriage that is destroying you, and you are in love with someone that walks away, and now a little life present needs you to take care of her for all of her needs when you're in despair trying

20

to take care of your own? Such a mess but beauty in the middle of it.

I can imagine mom thought, *all right, here is the oops baby and here is my demon-filled husband. No real father to put on the birth certificate but my husband's name; I must move forward.* So, here is where the accounts of stories I've gotten from my mom and family members start to get a little bit entangled; you know, after all, I am from a Hispanic family, and we don't tell our secrets! No matter what they are, we keep the secrets of the family to the point where I don't even know if everyone knows the truth, and if they do, maybe they will never admit to them or divulge it. I know that my mother has tried to make her life as comfortable as she could with the obstacles she's faced. She has never made very good choices when it comes to men in her life, and I have been taking the brunt of most of those things or at least, I've always felt that way in my life as a child. Very little, if ever, did I feel protected by her, my family, or even by strangers for that matter.

I know that when I was a baby, one of my mother's boyfriends or husband used to put liquor in my bottle so that I would sleep longer and not disturb him. Wow! I often think about how innocent, fragile, and tiny I was and how all I needed was comfort, love, and attention when I cried and instead, I was given rejection and liquor. I heard that my mom was with her husband for a little bit after I was born. I don't think he ever took kindly to me. From the bits and pieces of the story I was told, he abused my mother so badly it seems he was going to kill her. I'm certain that such experience for my mother not only added fear to her life and mine but also maybe drove a wedge between her maternal instincts and love for me because I am a source of pain for her.

21

My father was still not in the picture, nowhere to be found for the woman that he wooed and got pregnant. I'm sure my mother was angry, lonely, desperate, and felt undervalued. So, she kept on dating and another boyfriend she was dating when I was around a year and a half to two years dislocated my shoulders. I don't know why, was I reaching to be picked up? Was I clapping my hands too loud? Was I going in for a hug? Was I having a tantrum? I guess I will never really find out because I was not given a clear answer. Again, I feel the sting of rejection. Even as an adult, an answer was not provided. Am I still not worth giving the truth to? How did I feel when this happened to me? Did I cry like I am right now? Did I feel like I can't breathe like I feel right now? Did I run in pain? Did I lay on the ground and roll around in anguish? Did I run around in complete fear? Was I looking for my mommy, was she even there? I don't know, I may never know!

From what I was told, my mother broke up with this boyfriend for dislocating my shoulders. I was told that she said she would never go back to him again because of what he did. I was also told that he came over the house one day, begging for her to go back with him and she said no, so he jumped out of the third-floor window; he survived, and she never did return to him! In the middle of that mess, there was beauty…

All I hear about was that when I was little, I tried to get away from my mom's house often. It was said that my mom lived on one side of the street and my grandparents on the other side, and so I was always trying to cross the street even when I was little like two or three years old. There were times my mother would be looking everywhere for me and couldn't find me, but they would find me on my uncle's or aunt's bed, fast asleep. I often wonder about why a child

22

would react that way. Why run from your mommy's home? I know that one of those running away moments, I was hit by a van while crossing the street. Thank goodness the van wasn't going at high speed! I had a few bumps and bruises, but nothing major. It makes you wonder where my supervision was, and how was I able to constantly cross the street without an adult? Things that make you go hmmmm…

Did I feel unloved then? Was that the beginning of a root within me of always feeling like a black sheep and unloved by my parents, aunts, uncles, and family relatives?

Those stories are all mixed within what I've heard from aunts, uncles, and my mom, and little tiny glimpses here and there of my memory, but they're all mixed with everything I've been told. I do find it strange, but I have barely any memory before the age of four. I was told by a therapist once that kids can have a memory as early as two years old, I just don't have that. I've tried to talk to my mother about a lot of pain as a child especially those moments I can remember after the age of five, but she is in complete denial. I can't say that I blame her; it must be very painful to have someone tell you, *hey, you are the source or at least, in part, a source of my pain, can we talk about it?*

Denial just makes everything seem easy and tolerable for the person doing the denying. Who was there for me? Who was protecting me from the liquor in my bottle? From the abuse of my mother's boyfriend? How many times had he hurt me and either no one knew about it or didn't do anything until it got too far? Did I carry this with me throughout my youth into my adulthood? I did seem to have problems trusting people, always having this deep-down fear that sometimes, I cannot explain. Insomnia, worry, depression, anxiety, anger, and drastic mood swings affected me from my childhood to my adulthood.

23

My mom met my new stepfather when I was really young, maybe two years old. I don't remember much, but I do remember crying at the window for my mom all the time, as I watch her leave for her dates. This was in our apartment that was downstairs from my grandmother's house.

I was around three years old, and I have a glimpse of my mom being pregnant. I was having a baby brother and I was so excited. She asked me what his name should be and I said, "Frankie," she said okay, and everyone called my brother Frankie because I would yell at anyone who tried to call him anything else, even though that isn't his name. It's still the name everyone knows him by today.

My mother and her boyfriend were now officially together, and he moved in with us. I was spending a lot of time upstairs at grandma's house. Then we moved to Franklin Street in Stamford. He was a nice guy, and I really liked him. He used to take me outside and teach me how to dig for earthworms. Then we would take the plastic bucket full of earthworms and go the pier in Shippan beach in Stamford and go fishing. He taught me how to wrap the fishing wire around a glass bottle and at the end of the wire, tie a hook. Then he would tell me to get one of the worms, and I would happily grab one of the feisty worms, and he showed me how to put it on the hook so the fish would jump up out of the water to eat it. I was so excited to unwrap my fishing line from the glass bottle and toss it over my head into the water. I never could get it on the first few tries; I always had to do it harder and harder to have it go far enough in the water.

After a few trips to the pier, I was finally good enough to catch my first fish. He pulled the line, and I didn't know what to do, so my new father got behind me and showed me how to wrap the line around the bottle so I could

24

slowly pull up the fish. My first fish was not that big, but I was super excited; I did it! He praised me and said I did really good and he put it in a cooler he brought that had water in it so we could take it home and eat it. He also had a second cooler full of beer, that wasn't for fish. I Don't think my mom ever came with us on these fishing trips, but they were fun.

It wasn't very long before the fun fishing trips stopped and my beautiful brother's father became my monster. I don't remember why I started receiving quite a few pretty severe beatings by his hand. One I barely have a memory of, I must've been about four or five years old, and for whatever reason, he took a leather belt and the buckle and beat me so badly that my back was full of welts and some blood started coming out. My grandfather who only lived about maybe a quarter of a mile away came walking to my mom's house to take me out of that place. I'm not sure how he found out about this beating; I honestly have suppressed that memory. For some reason, I remember the emotion of that memory, but I'm completely blacked out on what the beating was and why I had to be beaten that way.

I'm so grateful for my grandfather. I see him as a tall tower of love, kindness to me, and savior. I tried to stay with my grandparents as much as possible; I was constantly back and forth to and from my grandparents' home. First grade at one school, then halfway through, I went to another school and then back to the first school. My grandfather used to walk me to school which was a block or two away at Rogers school; he used to time it so every time we were walking to the school, the bell would ring and he would say, "See, they rung the bell because the most beautiful girl in the school is coming." I looked forward to that every day; he would say it every day, and I wanted to hear it. It was so amazing to have him as a grandfather. When all my cousins would come over, we would play outside, and he would give us all quarters to go to the corner store and buy penny candies, then he would call me separately and give me a dollar and say, "Don't tell anybody, this is our secret." Then there were times he would have big bags of candy, mainly these gross jelly candies covered in sugar that he would offer all the kids when they came over. I hated those candies so he would hold some MaryJane's on the side for me; I loved those. My cousins would get so mad and jealous, but I believe he and I developed a special bond because he was the one always protecting me from my mom and stepfather.

My grandfather and I were inseparable, he would take me to the supermarket with him; he went every day walking to Grade A supermarket which was about a 20-minute walk, then he would take me to St. Mary's church which was on the way to the thrift store they had in their church basement, to let me pick out whatever game, toy or piece of clothing I wanted. It's because of him that I felt worthy of some love.

Even though when I was walking to school with him, it was special. I still had a hard time because, to me, school was always tough. I was always tired and felt like I couldn't focus. I was also born with a white patch on my eye, and a kid asked me what it was. I was self-conscious, and it seemed to be getting bigger and bigger over my eyelid. My mom took me to the Dr., and he couldn't figure it out. They did, however, find out that I had really bad anemia and had to be put on high doses of iron.

I felt ashamed at school a lot. I remember we were supposed to write a story for Father's Day. Well, I really didn't have a father. I had my grandfather, and I loved him like a father, but I knew he was my grandfather. I had an aunt that reminded me that they were not my parents, and my

26

parents didn't want me, the reason I was there, and that always crushed me inside.

I made up a Father's Day story that my Father was away traveling, and he brought me a koowala. The teacher asked if I meant a koala bear? I said yes, a real one that he got for me in Australia, and he has it in a cage in my house and I get to play with it. I remember writing it and thinking, it's not true, but I really want it to be true. I didn't want my teacher and classmates to know that I was lying; that I didn't have my dad around and that I didn't get anything much for holidays. It frustrated my 1st-grade teacher, so she asked me if I was stupid, I said "no, I'm not stupid," but that really hurt my feelings. I felt embarrassed that all the other kids heard her say that and now, they think I'm stupid too. I stayed back in 1st grade, and I carried the emotion of feeling stupid for most of my life. I switched back and forth to different schools and couldn't catch up. I was always switching my numbers and letters from how I saw them in my mind to how they were written on paper. I had lots of trouble concentrating, and I was distracted easily. I tagged it to my supposed stupidity.

Then to make things worse, I had to move back with my mom, and my mom moved further away from my grandparents to the other side of town to Greenwich Ave. We had another little baby brother now. He was so cute; his name was Edgar. I just love my brothers. I was about five or six years old. At this point, I remember feeling afraid but also loving my stepfather like he was my dad because even though he wasn't nice to me, he was the only dad I knew.

One day, he was playing with my brothers and lifting them up in the air with his feet like Superman and tickling them. It looked like so much fun; the boys were laughing so hard, so I said, *"I want to play, I want to play,"* and my stepfather said: "Come and play." I remember jumping like

27

"yay." I was so excited to play and be held up in the air by his feet like superman. So, I jumped up on the couch where he was laying on his back, and I hopped on his feet, and instead of him grabbing me and tickling me like my brothers, he grabbed me with one hand on my arm and with the other hand between my legs and squeezed my private area. I remember feeling afraid, and I didn't like that feeling. He held me tight, and I immediately jumped off. I said 'that's it, I don't want to play anymore; forget it." I sat on the floor and started pouting. He found that very funny and started laughing at me. I felt horrible, uncomfortable, and scared. He looked at me and beckon me to come and play. I said no, I don't like it. He laughed and asked if I was okay. I didn't answer him; I could feel my eyes getting watery. My baby brothers had no idea, so they said *yay* and kept on jumping on him like Superman. I remember hearing the clanking of pots and pans behind me in the kitchen. My mother was in there cooking, I believe.

I was so afraid; I didn't know what happened, but I know I didn't like it. I was confused. Why did he touch me like that? I don't want to play that game anymore. What's worse is that it didn't stop there. I think he saw this as an open-door opportunity, now that he touched me, and I was too scared to tell my mom what just happened because I wasn't even sure what did happen.

My mom used to work late in the evening cleaning offices, and he used to be drunk a lot, and I dreaded being home alone with him and my little brothers. I felt like it was my job to protect them. Then not soon after, the nightmare started. He used to come into my bedroom while I was sleeping. I can smell beer on his breath and in his skin, and he would put his hands down my pajama pants and my shirt, and I would press my legs together and shut my eyes really

28

tight, trying to act like I was sleeping so he can leave me alone. I would press my legs together with all of my might and my arms together with all of my might to be safe, but he was stronger than me. I don't know if any of this happened before these memories began because I honestly can't remember too many details before this age.

When he touched me, I waited for him to be gone, for my mom and me to be alone and said, *Mommy, Papi touched me down there*. She got down in my face, clenched her teeth together in fierce anger and said to me, "Stop being a liar, you better never say that again." I remember feeling completely numb as if my earth just shattered. I just swallowed hard, and my eyes filled up with tears; she turned and walked away. If she didn't believe me, who was going to believe me? Who was going to protect me? Where is grandpa?

I knew she really didn't believe me because she kept leaving us with him while she was going to work. He kept doing what he was doing at least a couple of times a week, that is what it felt like. Every time she left, the door would close, and I would instantly have so much distress; it would paralyze me in my tracks. My stomach hurt so bad, my muscles felt like they atrophied, and I would curl up in a ball on my bed, praying that he would not come to my room again, staring at the door until my eyes couldn't stay open any longer. When he did come into my room, there were times I had the strength to fight him off. He would get angry and make me get up at about 10 or 11pm and fry him some eggs. I remember being so small that I had to pick up the heavy cast-iron with both of my hands drag it half way and then grab a chair to put it on the stove, put a little oil in it and fry his eggs. I burned myself pretty badly one day because I took the hot oil in the pan and poured cold water on it to

29

clean the pan. He came running to help me because I started crying. When my mom got home, he told my mom I was trying to cook eggs. Hmmmm…I guess he forgot to mention it was for him and it was because he tried to molest me and was mad I didn't let him. He knew that what he did was wrong and also asking me to cook for him when I was so young.

I just remember always feeling so lonely and abandoned, feeling unsafe, uncovered, and insecure. Was he going to be in my room that night? Would I be woken up by a hand down my pants or my shirt? Or was it just a straight up beating? Even my older cousin, Maria, experienced something similar with him. She came to babysit us so my mom could go to work. He was home drinking as usual. When he got drunk, he tried to rape her. She fought him and she screamed; she got away from him and as she was escaping his grip, she broke a large piggy bank statue that was on the floor and hundreds of coins spread across the room. He came to his senses and realized what he was doing and stopped. She immediately called her mom and told her what just happened and even after all of that, nothing!!! Nothing was done!! Nothing! All I know is she didn't come to babysit us anymore.

I grew up in my mother's house and my grandparents' house. My grandparents' house was a blessing and a refuge that I believe now God gave me as a retreat or reprieve from the day-to-day nightmare of my stepfather and a mother who turned a blind eye. I was really without supervision; my grandparents really did love me. I knew that maybe they felt helpless, not strong enough to help or maybe they just didn't believe me either or acted like they didn't know. My grandparents' house was better than my mom's house, but I was terrified a lot there too. They had a landlord

30

name Nick, and he was an evil man in my eyes. I was absolutely in fear every time I saw him.

One day, I was sitting on the porch of my grandmother's house; it was a hot summer day, and there wasn't much to do. Nick stopped his truck in the driveway, jumped out of the truck, ran to the back of his truck and pulled out a machete, and started running after me saying, *I'm going to kill you, I'm going to kill you, you better run, or I'm going to kill you*! Oh, my God, I jumped up from the Porch steps, leaped onto the porch and then into the door which led to the hallway up the stairs to my grandparents' house. I remember feeling completely hopeless; I was completely shaking and crying, and I think I even wet myself. He thought it was completely hilarious, a funny joke to scare me every chance he got. Every time I saw his truck was home, I wouldn't come outside. Even as I write this, I remember my poor heart pounding in my chest and the fear that somebody's going to kill me. My grandparents just said he's not going to kill you, don't be afraid of him. But what no one understood is that I was constantly in fear at home in my mom's house, and now, I am afraid in my grandparents' house. Fear, anxiety, worry, and depression played a huge role in my upbringing. In a Hispanic's household, nobody talks about it, and nobody deals with it. Get over it, stop being a baby, is the motto. So, I was screwed!

Even though being at my grandparent's was scary at times because of Nick the landlord, my grandfathers' alcoholism, my grandparents fighting a lot, an uncle that was on some serious drugs and an angry and not so loving aunt, I still felt more loved there, and I loved being there way more than I did at my mother's house with my stepfather.

My grandparents' home was dysfunctional, but they played a big role in my upbringing. Besides telling me about

God, they introduce me to wrestling WWF. I used to love sitting there and watching it with them; it was one of my grandmother's favorite things to do. I used to love Andre the giant, Super Fly Jimmy Snucka and Hulk Hogan. I got into jumping off the arms of the sofa and on to the pillows or dolls as Super Fly did. There are some good memories there; I'm so glad I have them, and I treasure them very much.

I remember all the time that I lived and spent at grandma and grandpa's house. I would run home from school to make sure I caught Little House on the Prairie when it came on TV at 4 pm. There was no such thing as DVRs, so if you didn't catch the show, you missed it! Grandma made sure that we watched *The Price is Right* together and *Wheel of Fortune*. Then in the evening, when it came on, we watched *The Love Boat*, and a soap opera called *Dynasty*.

I remember many times coming home to grandma's and putting the first dial of the TV on U for universe, then slowly turning the second dial to try and get my favorite TV shows, which of course, included cooking shows with Julia child's and Jacques Pépin, art with Bob Ross and Mr. Rogers. I always wanted to be a chef on TV. I would open a box of Betty Crocker, cracking the eggs while talking to my imaginary audience about the ingredients and tried talking in Julia's accent, which I screwed up pretty bad, but it worked for me and my imaginary audience. I even made a lasagna as a child once with no instructions and everyone loved it, at least, that's what they said. Those were the moments of beauty in the middle of the mess.

Sometimes, when I lived with my grandparents, when I wasn't home for a long stretch, I used to get sad. I missed my mom, little brothers, but I knew that with their father, they were better off than I was with him. I do recall one summer for my birthday when I was staying at my

32

grandparents' home, and my mom brought me a cake. I was super excited, I mean who doesn't like birthday cakes? It was summer vacation, my cousins were over, and my mom put the candle on the cake. I took a deep breath to blow out the candle, and my mom says, "You better make a good wish because this will be the last birthday cake I will ever get you." I got so sad, my voice started trembling. I said, "Why mommy?" She replied, "Because you're too grown for birthday cakes now." I didn't understand why she would hurt me on my birthday. I didn't want to cry in front of my cousins, so I just blew out the candles, and we ate the cake. I think I was between 8-10 years old. I used to think she really didn't love me but I really wanted her to. She has kept her word; I never got another birthday cake from her.

As I sit down to write all these events, I'm getting flashbacks. My mother was the commencement of me not feeling loved, and my stepfather was always a huge part of both not feeling loved and my deep fears. I was always terrified of him; I do remember that feeling of terror and always having a knot in my stomach. It wasn't just the fondling, also the severe beatings and strict rules. He used to do some really messed up mind games.

I remember my mom used to run me a bubble bath, and a clawfoot bathtub. It was a small bathroom, but I remember the toilet used to be behind the tub. Once I got into the bath, he would come in and stand over my tub looking at me when I'm in the tub, and I would put my head down and just look at the bubbles, pretending he's not there, hoping he would go away. Then he would giggle, go behind me and start urinating in the toilet while making the sound of 'oooh' and 'ahhh's' as he's relieving himself in the toilet. I would just look at the bubbles or quietly play with a bath toy and try

33

to have the bubbles cover my chest, my little chest; I didn't want him to see.

When these events happened, sometimes, my mom would be home, and other times, he would just tell me I need to go and take a bath. But I couldn't say anything because if I did, I would be punished and I was a liar according to my mother, so I just sat in fear, hoping that I can get out of the tub quick enough to get dressed, praying that he doesn't come back in. I got really good at getting dressed, quickly grabbing my towel and swiftly going to my room before he calls my name to do something for him, whether it was picking up his shoes, making something to eat, changing my brothers' diaper, or putting my little brothers to bed. Whatever it was, I just didn't want to hear his voice.

One day, when I was sitting on the couch, and he sat next to me, terror came over me like a freezing blanket. He grabbed my hand and was trying to force it down his pants. I said no, refusing and kept pulling my hand and curling into a fist so I couldn't feel anything. I don't remember how long that lasted. I got away; he was so drunk that I was able to run to my room and he fell asleep on the couch. I don't know why I feel like this happened more than once, I just can't remember. The crappy thing about this apartment was that it was a train apartment, you had to go through each room to get to the other room, my room was right next to the living room, then my brothers' room in the middle, then the last room towards the front of the house was my parents' room. So, he always had access because our bedrooms didn't have doors; only his and mom's room.

He was a strange man and did some strange things. Once, he said, *watch, I want to show you something.* He'll set up a trap in the large garbage bins outside, wait for a pigeon to go in to get garbage and pull a rope which catches the bird inside. He will then put it in the cage and said, *see sweetheart, I got you a bird.* He caged the bird in the bathroom, that bird was always screeching and pooping everywhere. This gave him even more of an excuse to come to the bathroom when I was in the tub because he said he had to check on the bird. He would say, "Do you like the bird? I got the bird for you." I don't know if in his weird sick way, he was trying to be kind, trying to alleviate his guilt, or if this was just a sick way of having my trust and love him even though he was hurting me. I told him I didn't like the bird because the bird was messy and loud and not friendly, so he said I was just an ungrateful child, that I didn't appreciate anything he did for me. So, he got rid of the bird and let me know it was my fault; I felt terrible about it.

I'm sure I didn't do everything right or obediently, but I was scared to do anything wrong. I tried to occupy myself with trying to be protective over my little brothers. They meant everything to me; they brought me sanity and love. My first little brother, Frankie, was diagnosed with leukemia when he was about three years old. My mom was constantly at Yale Children's hospital with him getting blood transfusions and spinal taps. It sure stressed my mother out more than anything else going on in her life. I don't remember too much of his illness because a lot of it was kept from me; you know, adult business, not for children to know. I remember one day begging my mom to let me go with her to the hospital for one of my brother's spinal tap appointments. I asked if I can please skip school because I really wanted to go. My mother finally caved in and let me go. She gave my brother to the doctors, and he was screaming to the top of his lungs. They strapped him face down on the table, and then my mom quickly grabs me and took me outside of the room and into the waiting area. I can

35

hear my brother screaming mommy and crying so loud that I wanted to go and rescue him. I curled up in a corner and covered my ears because I didn't understand what they were doing to him. I never went back again to another visit; it traumatized me.

During the last-ditch efforts of the doctors, they told my mother it was time to make funeral arrangements for her baby boy. She said absolutely not, went to a local church, and at a service started weeping and crying and asking the Lord to heal her son. When the people at the church saw my mother in the back crying, they asked her what was wrong, and she told them. They prayed over my little brother and miraculously that is exactly what the Lord did. He started to get better, and when my mother took my little brother back to the hospital, they couldn't explain how he was better. The Lord healed my little brother from leukemia. I am so grateful to God for saving my brother and healing his body! He is now a full-grown man.

I'm sure the pressure of my little brother being ill had made me even more of a target for stress release. My stepfather would blame me for everything the boys did. If they broke something, I would get the beating because I should've been watching them. If they cried, why wasn't I doing something to make them stop crying? As we started to get older, the boys were allowed to go outside, and if I wanted to go outside too, it was usually an issue. I always felt like I had a bulls-eye on my back that made me the prime target. I started to feel afraid to let my brothers do anything that would hurt them because it would definitely hurt me. I was overprotective of them; I was constantly watching over them; I felt like their mom even though I was little also.

One day, my brothers wanted to go outside to play and we were running around the house playing tag. It was a

36

nice day outside, and mom said we can go outside. The boys ran out the door, and when I tried to follow them outside, my stepfather grabbed my long ponytail and wrapped it around his hand and yanked me really hard, and it snapped my neck back. He pulled me into the house and said I wasn't going anywhere. My head and neck hurt so bad I just started crying, and I went to my room. I was so angry and frustrated, but my mom said nothing and I was too afraid to say anything. It just was so unfair! It made me feel like my brothers were so special and loved and I wasn't, but why? I didn't do anything wrong? So, I started to feel like I was starting to resent my brothers. Even though they were little and didn't know any better, but they knew I would get in trouble if I did anything. So, when they were mad, they made sure they said I did it. Of course, being as young as they were, they had no idea about what I was going through.

I will always remember the beating of a lifetime that I received from my stepfather. I was always fatigued, and I've always had trouble sleeping because of the fear I was having of waking up to my stepfather over my bed or his hand down my pajamas. So, to get up in the morning was a serious challenge. My mother would practically have to throw water on me for me to get up and she did that several times. We lived at the bottom of a very long hill and our bus stop, of course, was way at the top of the hill. This particular morning, when I got up, I realized I was behind schedule, my mother tried to wake me up several times, but I just couldn't get up. Finally, I woke up, I got dressed, and I ran out of the house as fast as I could to go up the hill and catch the bus. As I turned a corner of the hill, I saw the bus at the bus stop all the way at the top. I started running with all my might as fast as I could; the bookbag full of books was hitting my back, but to no avail, the bus driver didn't see me, and he drove away.

Holy crap! I miss the bus, what am I going to do now? I was completely paralyzed by fear; I started crying and walking back down the hill contemplating what I was going to do. Oh, my God!!! I decided I'll go to my mom's friend's house who lives two houses from us and tell her that I missed the bus. When I went to her house; it was early in the morning, so she opened the door half-asleep and said, *what are you doing here*? I told her I missed the bus, that if I go home, I'll be in so much trouble with my father. That I was so scared I don't know what to do. She said, *well, we need to call your mother and let her know because you're supposed to be in school, so, you can't stay here all day.* I pleaded with her not to call because I'm afraid he's going to be really mad. I could feel my legs shaking and my stomach starting to hurt. She said well, we'll call your mother and see what she says. I implore her to call my mother and tell her; that I can't do it. So, she called my mother's house; I pressed my ear up against the phone; I heard my mother pick up the phone, and when the neighbor explained to her that I was at her house, my mom whispered, *keep her there for a little bit, he's on his way to work.* As soon as she said that, my stepfather picked up the other phone line and heard everything. He started yelling, *what do you mean she missed the bus? Tell her little ass to get home right now!* My mother's friends said, okay, I'll send her home. She hung up the phone, looked at me and said, *I am so sorry, but you have to go home.* I started crying and grabbing her, saying, *please don't send me home, can't I just stay here?* She said *no, I'm sorry, you have to go home. You're going to be fine; don't worry about it.* So, I grabbed my bookbag and started walking just a house over. My heart was pounding; I was feeling nauseous, stomach pain, and

38

walking as slow as I can. I knew by hearing him on the phone that I was going to be in for it. We lived on the third floor, so I took my sweet time going up the stairs. When I got to the top of the stairs, he was standing in the doorway. I'm sure I turned white because I felt blood leave my face. He grabbed me by my hair, pulled me into the house, took off his construction steel toe boot and started beating me so badly that the first hit knocked the wind out of me, and I couldn't even get the first scream out.

Then slam, I fell to the floor; I could barely breathe. I looked up, my mother was in the living room where he was beating me; she was folding the clothes she just washed. I remember that because as he persistently hit me with his boot, I dragged myself over to her, grabbed on the towel she was folding and called out for her. I gasped and reached out for her help. He grabbed me by my legs and dragged me closer to him; my mom then snatched the towel out of my hands, turned around and kept folding the clothes. She let him continue the beating to the point where he was exhausted, and I could not stand on my own feet. After he was done beating me, he put on his boots and told me I better never miss that bus again. I just laid on the floor sobbing and holding myself; I felt broken. When he was walking out of the house, he walked over to my mom and gave her a goodbye kiss, as if he just did a job well done. Once he left, my mother waited a few minutes and then picked me up and brought me to my room. I remember hobbling and couldn't stand straight. She told me to go to bed, but I couldn't lay down because I was so sore and in pain. All I can think of was I hated my life, and I wanted to die.

Mom and I spent the day at home, and my mother's neighbor came by to see if everything was okay and saw that I was beaten very badly. She told my mom she should've just

39

let me stay at her house no matter what. My mom said it would've been worse if I let that happen. I stayed in my room the whole day just sitting there. I was praying he wouldn't come home, but he did, and when he came home that night from work, he came into my room and said, "I'm sorry I had to hit you like that, but you missed the bus; don't miss the bus ever again."

That is just a few of the many beatings by the hand of my stepfather. There were so many that I can't even account for them all. I just remember things like when he used to beat me and then make me sleep sitting down as a punishment. I would have to go into my room, sit at the edge of my bed, and sleep that way. Then my mom would wait for him to get drunk and go to sleep, then she would come into the room and lay me down; she would have to wait for him to be asleep soundly or she would also be beaten. This went on for a long time. Unfortunately, my brothers also started to become a little bit of targets for him as well. They were also getting hit all the time, not as bad as me, but I hated the fact that I couldn't protect them. Then there were times he was beating my mother, and I would have to try and entertain the boys so that they didn't hear mom screaming and crying and him calling her such horrific names while he was unmercifully beating her. When I started to get older, I just couldn't take it anymore. I had a plan; I will get a big knife, and while everyone is sleeping, I will sit by my mother's bedroom and as soon as he gets up to go to work, I am going to kill him. That's the only way this will end, and we will be free. So, I acted like I was sleeping and I got the knife and sat by the door. I fell asleep, and my mother got up before him and saw me sleeping by their bedroom door with the small utility knife. She grabbed it out of my hand and said, *what are you doing? Are you crazy? If he sees you, he will hurt*

40

you. She picked me up and put me to bed before he would notice anything. I said, *mom, please just leave him, why are you still with him*? She would tell me to mind my own business and not get involved. She thinks I'm crazy, but she's still with this monster. I tried hard to get out of that house and live with my grandparents as many times as I could.

They were my sanity, which is funny when they do have issues and would fight all the time but not physically. It was more of arguments. But damn, did I feel loved there! My grandmother was a tough cookie, and my grandfather was an alcoholic at night and an amazing grandfather by day. I couldn't stay with him all the time because I wasn't their daughter even though I felt like they were more my parents than the parents I had.

My stepfather, as mean and violent as he was, he was really the only father I knew, so I call him Papi. My biological father started coming around as I got a little older. I liked him; he was a nice guy, just not a good father, not to me anyway. When I was younger, I used to be terrified of my biological father because there was one time he came by my mother's house and saw me playing outside and said, *hi, how are you? You remember who I am right*? He said *I'm your father*. I said *yes, I know*, and then I heard my name, and when I looked up, my stepfather was leaning out the window and told me to get my ass upstairs. I told my biological father that I had to go. He asked if I was ok, I simply told him I have to go. My stepfather knew who my biological father was; he got so outrageously mad and beat me for talking to him. When my mother asked why he was hitting me, he told my mother that I was stepping into the street instead of staying on the sidewalk like he said. She believed him; it justified the beating because I wasn't obedient. I was just so confused about what just happened. Let's just say every time

41

my biological father would come around to show me his big rig truck or his motorcycle, I would completely panic and tell him I can't talk, that I have to go. I never understood why my biological father never just told my mom he wanted to spend time with me and get visitation rights. Instead, he left me to the wolves.

People who used to come to our home, and the ones that were friends with my mom and the family, knew of the abuse, at least the physical beatings, so they would be extra kind to me, and bring me toys or candy or ask my mom if I can go to their house and hang out. Now that I think about it, a lot of times, my mom did let me go to the neighbor's house or my grandparents' house or my cousins' house. I think is so that I wouldn't get abused. She was probably terrified herself because he was a very abusive man even to my mom. For a very long time span, he was my monster, a giant that I couldn't overpower because he was the adult. But in reality, he's only about 5 feet tall and maybe 120 pounds soaking wet. As I started to get older, I started to get better at wearing extra clothes at night, stronger at pushing him off, and I think I started to get too big for him to keep beating me the way he wants. He would definitely still pull my hair as hard as he could, but I started to build a resilience to it. Oh, don't get me wrong, I was still very afraid of him. I just got good at knowing my enemy and his tactics.

When I was about 8-9 years old, my brother was around 7 years old, and my baby brother was around 4 years old; we've moved on to the projects. First day in the bungalows in the village which is what we called the housing project we lived in. I went outside to play and got jumped by a black girl that wrapped my hair around her hands, punched me in the face from behind a few times. I tried to hit her back but she was behind me. I think I only landed like one or two punches.

Then I ran into the house and was absolutely terrified to go outside. So, not only was I terrified to be in my house, but now I was also terrified to be outside of my house. This young girl and her group of friends followed me home and waited outside, punching their fist to their hands, saying we'll get you when you come outside. I was so scared! My mom asked the reason for my fear. *Are those girls messing with you?* I said yes, she said well, you can't stay inside all day. Well, I did stay inside all day. I was so scared. The next day, I peered out the window, and I didn't see anybody, so I went outside. It took about two weeks, but finally, there I was face-to-face with the scariest girl in the village. I stood there for a second in fear. What was I going to do? My brain was saying run, but I just couldn't move my feet, so I lifted up my fist and said okay, let's do it! I was fatigued and I couldn't be hiding in my house anymore. She said, *great, it's about time I was wondering when you were going to stop being afraid, now we can be friends. You can't come and live in these projects and be a punk. You need to learn how to fight and defend yourself.* Boy, I was relieved! I thought I was in for an ass-kicking again. We became friends; she was actually pretty cool, and she taught me how to fight. I then started meeting more really great people that were neighbors, and we all became friends playing double Dutch, hopscotch, and basketball. I spent as much time outside as I could.

Things at home, of course, weren't getting any better. My father was very abusive to my mother and now my brothers even more. He was always drunk, vulgar, and a monster. I started noticing that my mother was making friends with some of the Hispanic neighbors as well. And some of the friends that she had were starting to get to know us, and I liked them, especially this one man who was always very kind.

One day, on a hot summer day, my stepfather started beating my mother in the middle of the day, so I took my brothers and quickly put them in our bedroom. They were so scared and started crying. I closed the door and started singing to them so they couldn't hear the screams and the beatings downstairs. Once they calmed down a little, I then went downstairs quietly to see if my mom was okay and saw my stepfather was grabbing my mom's arms because in defending herself, she had ripped the phone from the wall and was trying to beat the crap out of him. I ran up the stairs, leaned out the bedroom window, called on my mother's new friend, and said to him, *please, help my mom, he's beating her, and I'm afraid he's going to kill her*! He came closer to my window and instructed me to open the door for him so he can help. I said I can't, that I'm terrified he will beat me too if I do that. My mother's friend said I should just open the door and he will handle the rest. So, I told my brothers to stay in the room and locked the door, and I ran downstairs as fast as I could, ran to the door, swung it open and ran back up the stairs. My mother's friend came in and beat the crap out of my stepfather like he was a rag doll, and threw him out and told him to get the hell out of the house. My stepfather said, *don't tell me what to do; this is my house*, but my mother's friend didn't listen and told him to get the hell out. My mother was crying. I ran back up to check on my brothers, and by the time I came back down, my stepfather was gone. I was so happy! I got that monster out of my house and away from us and away from my mom. Monster gone…right?

For a few weeks, we were so at peace at home. My mom, of course, was still fatigued, but now, she was starting to date that nice man, so we were kind of left to our own devices. I was out in the backyard playing all day long, all

44

evening long, into the early morning hours. It was freedom! Even though our mother beat the crap out of us when we didn't do what we were supposed to do, it was nothing compared to the monster. At this point, I was about 10 or 11 years old, and I remember being outside till 2 o'clock in the morning and I came inside, and I said to my mother: "Mom, don't you think you should be telling me to come inside? It's 2 o'clock in the morning?" She said you don't listen to me anyway, so I don't bother. I said, *just tell me what to do. You don't listen anyway, so go to bed*, was her reply. It felt kind of crazy going from really strict and horrible supervision to absolutely no supervision.

I don't know how long it took, but it wasn't very long before my mother's new friend was spending a ton of time at our home and moved in. I started noticing my mother cooking more when he was there, and she seemed happier.

This was going to be different; this guy seems really nice. One fond memory I have in the beginning with him was that he used to make amazing houses out of popsicle sticks. He would ask my brothers and me to go around the neighborhood and collect as many popsicles sticks as we could find. He would take them all, clean them really well then sand them down to take off the colors that were staining them from the frozen, sugary ice pop that once surrounded them. Then for hours, we would watch him as he would build a foundation out of sticks by gluing them together, then the side walls, then the roof. But before he fully glues the roof, he would take Christmas lite bulbs and wire them in the home. Separately, he took sticks and made furniture for the house like tables, chairs, beds and things a real home would have. It was so fascinating seeing what popsicle sticks can become with imagination and skills. Then he would put the roof on, let it all dry well then, he would plug it in, and the

45

home would have lights inside, and you could see the furniture and the details. He even made some of the homes with operating doors and windows. Real looking windows that I think he used plastic to make them. We weren't allowed to play with the houses. Although we tried every time he wasn't home. They were so cool and I wanted to learn how to make them, but he never showed me how to do it.

She soon became pregnant with my little sister, and we now became the 'other' children. I used to always feel that way especially when my little brothers were born, and their father started abusing me. But now, my little brothers were getting treated badly as well. It wasn't long when my new stepfather started to become really controlling and not very nice, especially to my little brothers. He started being such a bully to them. He would hit them, punish them, and make them serve him as if he were a king. It would piss me off to no end. He would come home from a long day of work and make my little brothers get on their knees to take off his boots and socks which smelled like raw eggs and a garbage cans full of dead fish. I hated that he did that to them. I told my mom to make him stop, but as usual, nothing! So, I started to tell my little brothers to fight back. I told them that every time he asked them to do something, just say no and if they had to, run. *He is not your father*, I would say; you don't have to listen to him anymore! But they were little and scared, so it was very hard for them to stop doing what he said because they were afraid of being beaten, and he was a bully. My youngest brother started fighting back; he was standing his ground even though he was scared. So, this stepfather started targeting my brother, Frankie, who was more fragile and innocent because of the terrible leukemia that almost took his life when he was a toddler. Making him do all of the dirty work because I wasn't doing it, now my little brother Edgar wasn't doing it either. I was so furious; my insides were exploding. I would say no, he doesn't have to do that for you, but because my little brother was so young and fragile, he would just do it anyway.

Then my little sister was born in 1982; she was the cutest little thing, and in their eyes, she could do no wrong. He and my mom would not allow us to play with her, be around her, and barely let us give her kisses and hugs. We were now the no-good stepchildren, and she was the precious princess born from the heavens and obviously, better than us. At least, that is how they made us feel.

So, in 1983, I went back to live with my grandparents for a while because being home was just no fun and getting worse. My mom literally wouldn't cook unless her man was coming home so my brothers and I would eat cereal or sugar sandwiches. Yes, you heard me right. Wonder bread dipped in sugar, and we would suck on ice cubes covered in Kool-Aid and sugar.

It wasn't that way at my grandparents' home; they were always cooking and had enough for any company that would come over. My grandfather was a great cook and did most of the cooking in the house. At least, at their house, I knew there would be something better to eat all the time. At their house, I always felt freer and more loved. I was getting seriously into breakdancing, and I was really good at it. I started watching every show I could and made up my own moves, popping, waacking and locking, and crazy footwork. Someone told a NY crew about me, and a few of the members came to Stamford, CT to check me out. They put on some music, and I freestyled for them in the middle of the street. They were the infamous Rock Steady Crew, and they were about to make a movie called Beat Street and needed a female dancer; they wanted me to join them in NY for rehearsals and the filming. I was so excited. I told them I needed permission from my mom because I had to go to school, they said okay. But when I told my mom, she said absolutely not, I cannot go to NY. I don't care what it's for. I wept profusely; I felt so disappointed! Then when the movie came out in 1984, I went to go see it, and my heart was broken that I wasn't in it with them, such an awesome opportunity I missed. It still hurts a little.

So, back home to my mom's I went. As my little sister was getting older, she was around two years old. She knew she could do no wrong. Well, one day, my mother reprimanded my little sister for bad behavior, and my new stepfather hit my mother for the first time in their relationship. He looked at me because I asked him what did you do to my mom; my mom looked at me and told me to mind my business, and he raised his hand to backhand me. So, I stuck my chest out and said, "Go ahead. I know where you sleep; I am not my mother. If you ever hit or lay a hand on me, I will cut your throat from ear to ear," while I made the motion with my hand across my throat. I was scared, but I was absolutely terrified of letting this happen to me again. Being abused by my mother's boyfriends and my ex-stepfather was enough. He saw the look on my face and knew I was serious about my threat, so he backed off and just told me to get out of his face.

So now, I had to try and protect my brothers; they meant so much to me! This guy was never a sexual predator or pedophile, thank God, not to me anyway, but he was cruel with his words, cruel with the belt, a drug addict, an alcoholic, and a gambler. My mother suffered greatly and for many years at his hand. He even threatened to kill her with a knife to her throat a few times.

48

Now, my little sister was even off-limits to her own mother reprimands or discipline in any way. She was such a beautiful little girl, and also almost died when she was a baby, which is probably why she became untouchable for all of us. They became unbearably overprotective; it alienated us from her. But God is good, and she was also healed.

My mom was still with my sister's father for many years; he was becoming worse with erratic behaviors. He was on some serious drugs, drinking and would be out of the house for days at a time with no explanation. I needed to get out as soon as I could, so I went to the Stamford Mall and applied for a job at A&W Rootbeer fast food restaurant, but even though I was only 12 years old, I lied on the application and said that I was 16 years old. I looked 16 anyway. They believed me, so I started working, and I think I was making $3.50-$4.00 an hour, but I was determined to go to school and work as long as I could to make some money. My mother thought it was a great idea that I worked, that way I can give her the money, so she didn't fight me on it. My sister's father could care less what I did; I think he was just happy I wasn't around. My little paychecks were cashed at the restaurant by the manager, and I would keep a few bucks and give the rest to my mom. It wasn't long though before someone reported me, and I lost my job for lying on the application.

Chapter 2

THROUGH MY TEENS….

All of these events that happened and those I didn't even mention, prepared me for being a teenager, right? Yeah, right…A rejected, angry, lonely, worthless, pissed-off teenager.

I was so accustomed to living both at my mother's house and my grandparents' house. If I could, I would've stayed with my grandparents all of my life, but they wouldn't have it, and my mom would ask me to come back home because she was my mother. When my first stepfather, the "monster" moved away, it did make it easier to start developing a somewhat relationship with my biological father, Paul. Did I mention he was handsome? When I started to get to know him, I really enjoyed being around him. He would only come a few times a year and sometimes would surprise me with a motorcycle ride. That would happen at my grandmother's house, not my mom's. I wanted to love him more, get to know him more, and sometimes leave with him so maybe life could be better, but it never happened.

In the summer of 1986, I was excited because I hadn't seen him for a while, and my birthday was coming. He only came on my birthday and Christmas, and I knew that he would have a gift for me. Then I look up, and I see my grandmother and my aunt holding hands, asking each other who should tell me. I asked them, *tell me what*? Then they told me that my father had died the year before on August 25th. I didn't know what to say; I just said okay. I was watching TV with my uncle and acted as if I was very interested in the movie, which I think was the original

Superman. Inside, I felt crushed, heartbroken, but I acted like it was no big deal. That night, I crawled into bed and cried myself to sleep. Even though my biological father and I never really established a strong bond, I did love him. Besides my grandfather, he was very kind to me.

A few weeks before this, I had met a really cute boy. He was older than me; he was 17, and I was 13, but going on 14 years old in a few weeks. I have to say about this point, I was fully developed. I have gotten my first period at 11 years old. I was already wearing a C cup, and I was curvy in all the right places. This young man had a girlfriend his age, and her parents were super strict, so she was always in the house. I saw this as an opportunity to steal him away. I remember being at the back of the school, my friends and I had a beatbox, and I was playing the cassette of Salt and Pepa, "I'll take your man" there. I was Chilin in the parking lot of the school. He was sitting in front of his girlfriend's house talking to her, and I started singing loudly with my girls, "Salt and Pepa's back and we come to out rap you, so get out my face before I smack you. Ho, don't you know? Can't you understand? If you mess with me, I'll take your man."

His girlfriend got mad and was like, little girl, please. And her mother called her in, and he came over to talk to me. We quickly started having chemistry. I never had a boyfriend before, this felt nice. We talked for a couple of weeks, and he saw me after school crying and asked me what was wrong, so I told him I just found out that my dad died. He said I'm so sorry to hear that and held me in his arms. I just love the way he felt. He felt safe, loving, real, and strong. I told him if he wanted to be my boyfriend, he had to break up with his girlfriend. He said it was kind of hard because he was afraid of hurting her even though he didn't have feelings for her like that anymore. But I wanted him so bad that I kept

52

pushing for him to break up with her if he wanted to be with me. We kept seeing each other behind her back and finally, she couldn't take it anymore and broke up with him. Wow, I had a boyfriend, an older boyfriend. I could be out late, hang out and chill at my friends until dark and no one said anything.

The difference was that at my grandmother's house, I have to be home by dark while at my mother's house, it didn't matter at all what time I was home. So, when I was back-and-forth from my mother to my grandmother, my boyfriend would come to see me because he had a car. I quickly fell in love with his charisma and his attention to me, buying me things, telling me he loved me, being sweet all the time. He had me wrapped around his finger.

So, it took no time, and we went to a mutual friend's house where everybody used to hang out and hook up. He told me that he loved me and he was my first love, so he took my virginity. I was scared; my ex-stepfather used to try with fondling, but it never got far enough to penetrate, so this is my first "real love" sexual experience. It was painful and not fun at all. Like a week after this, he told me he didn't want to be with me anymore. I started to cry because my world came to an end. My heart was completely crushed, as I turned to walk away, he grabbed me and said, "I'm only playing; I wanted to see if you cared about me for real." I didn't like that at all, that was painful, he said he was sorry, so all was forgiven. Our relationship continued.

About one or two months after we started dating, we were hanging in the park with some friends, a friend of ours gave me a Walkman to listen to a tape. My boyfriend wanted to listen to it, so I told him to hold on for a few seconds. All of a sudden, I felt a pain in my back. He punched me really hard that it took my breath away. I said what the f**k is

53

wrong with you. He said, the next time I tell you I want something, you better listen. I said oh, no way. I turned to walk home, and he followed me home, telling me I just need to listen. He didn't mean to hit me so hard. He was sorry, so our relationship continued.

I loved him so much that these weren't warning signs to me; they were normal. He was so sweet most of the time. We were still having sex, having fun, hanging out, playing basketball in the park with friends and all the things teenagers do when they are in love. He was in high school, and I was in middle school. He was always doing such cute things like picking me up from school, taking me to the movies, buying me flowers, taking me out to eat and all the cute stuff a good boyfriend does. He used to work at the gas station in Darien, so he also taught me how to drive his car which was a stick shift so that I can be with him at his job, hang out, and he would buy me scratch-offs so I can try and win. Although I was 13 turning 14, I used to drive all over town with him and without him; he trusted me to drive his car.

It wasn't long before our relationship was volatile. I was spending time at my grandmas as much as possible because he lived up the street and the hookup house was also up the street.

A few months into our relationship, we got into a huge argument, so I broke up with him. My friend June, at the time, asked me to go to the pizza place in the neighborhood and he saw me. I was walking away with my girlfriend and he ran behind me and kicked me in my back. I fell to the ground and badly scraped my knees, and they started bleeding, and the palms of my hands got little rocks stuck in them. My girlfriend picked me up and suggest we keep on walking; she was shaking and I was crying. He ran

54

back as if getting ready for a race and ran up with all his might and kicked me again behind my knees; again, I fell down. She picked me up and started yelling at him to stop. He ran back again and did it again. At this point, I could barely walk. My friend said she was calling the police, and he stopped but kept mocking me and laughing that I was hurting. When we got to her home, I was in so much pain, but we kept it from her mom. I waited for him not to be around, then I walked to my grandmother's house.

He kept coming outside my grandparents' home and my mom's home looking for me. My mother told me he was there. I didn't tell anyone what he did to me; I loved him and I was embarrassed.

A few days later, he found me and brought me flowers and asked me to forgive him. He said he loved me so much that he was so mad that we broke up and that I wouldn't talk to him. He was sorry, so our relationship continued. But now, I was starting to fear.

At this point, my grandparents had had it with me because of all the crap I was going through with him and my behavior when he was abusing me, so she told me to go back to my mom's. He didn't let up; the abuse was getting really bad. Now, we had a mutual friend where we hung out all the time that was near my mom's house. One day, he beat me so bad I could barely move. He threw me to the ground, jumped on me and said no one loved me, that's why my father never claimed me, my stepfather abused me, and my mother doesn't love me. Then he whipped out his penis and peed on me, and said that's what I am, a toilet. I just laid there in shock and embarrassment. I couldn't believe what just happened. I couldn't move; I couldn't scream; I couldn't talk. The pain was so deep physically and emotionally. After a long while, I got up, went to the bathroom, broke a shaving

55

razor and took out the razor, but as I was looking at my wrist to cut them, I just couldn't do it, so I looked in the cabinet and drank a whole package of allergy medication. He knew it wasn't good when I didn't come out of the bathroom. He knocked the door down, and when he saw the package of pills, he put his hand down my throat and made me throw up. I wanted it to be over! I didn't want to live anymore!! How would I ever be able to live knowing this boyfriend that I love so much keeps doing this to me? He felt really bad about this, and he was sorry, so our relationship continued.

It was and still is one of the most painful experiences of my life. Even as I write this, I had to keep pausing to wipe my tears away.

Our volatile relationship continued, and when I was in the 8th grade about to graduate, I realized I wasn't feeling well. I was throwing up all the time and very tired. Someone in school asked, *are you pregnant*? Oh, no, am I pregnant? I saw my boyfriend after school and told him, so we went to planned parenthood to get a free test because there was no way I was going to tell anyone I was pregnant. I was only 14 years old and about to start high school!

Shit! The test came out positive. Oh my God! What am I going to do? I ran to my mom's friend's house and told her everything and that I needed her to come with me to tell my mom because I was scared of what she and my stepfather would do to me. My mom's friend went with me, and we called my mom to the room. I told her to say it because I was petrified. My mom said, *I knew it, I just knew it, now you have no choice but to marry him, quit school and get a job.* She went out of the room, told my stepfather, and he started calling me names, whore, stupid, you name it. Both of them stop speaking to me for months. I was all alone. My grandmother said no, you're not coming here pregnant. No one at my home was speaking to me, and my boyfriend was a complete asshole.

The beatings didn't stop. When I was about 4-5 months pregnant, he threw me down the stairs. When my stomach started showing, he made sure he only punched me in the back, arms, legs or my face. He was considerate, so he didn't hit my stomach. After one of these beatings, I remember looking up from my bed and screaming to the top of my lungs, *God, why do you hate me so much? Where are you? I hate you!* I felt so unloved, alone and pathetic, abandoned by my family, boyfriend, and my God.

I tried to leave my boyfriend a few times. But it was really more terrifying leaving him than it was staying with him. When I would leave him, I would be walking, and he would just pop out of a tree or behind a car and chase me down to beat me. It was just safer knowing where he was. He would act as if he would regret it but if it weren't for me getting him mad, he wouldn't act that way. Then come the flowers, tears of sorrow, beatings, the pattern of our "love" story continued.

As the weeks went on, I started feeling the baby kicking inside of me. It was the weirdest but most comforting feeling I've ever had in my life. My son's father continued his abuse on every level, physically, mentally, and socially. He made sure to embarrass me at any opportunity he got in a social setting, calling me fat, a whore, stupid, and a bitch, just to name a few. When we were in a private setting, he would tell me that this baby better be his because if it's not, he will kill the baby and me and that I better not pay more attention to the baby than to him because he was here first.

I remember he used to have a car that the door on the passenger side was messed up, so in order to get in the car, you had to pull it really hard, then when you got in the car,

57

you have to lift the door, and it was heavy, and then pull it toward you as fast as possible in order for it to lock. I remember that so clearly because when I was about eight and a half months pregnant, I asked him to please open the door and to close it for me because it was really heavy. He used the F-word on me, that he is not my slave and I should do it myself. So, I struggled to open the door, got into the car and pulled the door as hard as I could, and I got a strong pain in my stomach. I started complaining, and he told me to shut up and that nothing better happen to the baby. Then as we were driving, heading towards my cousin's house, there was a skunk crossing the street, so I told him to slow down so that the poor animal can cross the street. He said yeah, watch this. He accelerated the engine and ran over the animal. I felt the tires in the car wobble as he went over the animal with his front passenger and rear passenger tires. I started crying. He started laughing at me. I was so upset and distraught because my son's father was a freaking animal; a beast, a horrible human being, a complete asshole who would kill an innocent animal. The justice in that was that his car smelled like skunk for months, I had such inner joy about that. In the mess, there was beauty.

All of these months, my mom and my stepfather still weren't speaking to me. My grandparents barely spoke to me; my aunts and uncles were all talking about me in a bad way; my cousins weren't around, and I had no friends. I was seriously alone, and all I could do was talk to my baby in my stomach, sing to my baby every day and every night. I would take my headphones and put it around my belly so he can hear the same music I was listening to. I couldn't wait to love this little guy or girl and have them love me back for real!!

My son's father had some very short moments of being kind and loving. Where he would run out and get me

Pizza and banana boats because that's what I wanted when I was pregnant. As long as I agreed to everything and wasn't combative and didn't show too much joy, then he was a pleasure to be around. My mom let him sleep over a lot; I guess she must have figured that, what was the point? So, he and I used to sleep on the floor in the living room. My stomach was so big, and so it caused me a lot of pain in my body and my stomach to sleep on the hard floor, my mother didn't want me sleeping on the couch, so I had no choice. My baby's father used to try to make a comforter bed for me to lay on. And there'll be times when he would say you're so beautiful; I like watching you sleep. And that, of course, would make me love him, forgive him, and see that there is a potential hope to be happy with him.

Then nine months was here and on January 27, 1988, I woke up in some serious pain. It felt better to die than to feel these contractions. I called up the stairs to my mom and said, *mom, I am in serious pain*. She told me to have a glass of warm milk, and I should inform her if there are changes. I said, okay. So, my son's father made me a glass of warm milk, and I drank it, and within 30 minutes, the pain was out of control. So, she said great, it's time. We got into my baby's father's car, and we went to the hospital. I was in labor for about six hours. While I was in labor, my mother was trying to sit there and comfort me but she couldn't, my son's father tried to comfort me but couldn't. All I wanted was to have the pain done with. When it was time for me to start pushing, my son's father was in the room. After the whole thing and my son came out, my son's father looked at him and said, *that is an ugly baby, I know that's not my son. He's too white and he's ugly*. The nurse said, *sir, he was just born, he doesn't have color yet, and he's beautiful*. All I can feel was heartbreak that this piece of shit was my son's

59

father. Then he proceeds to say I'm going to get a DNA, that's not my son. Part of me wished it weren't so that I can leave with my baby and never come back. My precious boy was 7lbs 9oz. 19" long, he named him Ernest.

Three days later, it was time to bring my baby home. My mother was super excited to have a new baby in the house, and my stepfather started speaking to me because he absolutely fell in love with Ernie. Of course, his father had nothing ready for the baby or me, so he had to go out and get a car seat before they would allow me to carry the baby home. When I got out of the hospital, we took the baby to his mother's house. And then he and I had to go get diapers, a diaper bag and some other necessities that he didn't get while I was in the hospital. I remember feeling extremely lightheaded and nearly passing out. Here I am, 15 years old, with an infant, a stupid ass, abusive 19-year-old boyfriend, and no idea what I am doing and what I am going to be doing with my life.

When my baby was about a week old, we took the baby to my cousin's house that lived on the other side of the projects. It was freezing, snowing and slippery, and my son's father and I got into a huge argument at my cousin's house. So, when I told him to just take me home, that it's freezing outside and the baby is only a week old, and he might get sick from the cold, he said: "Nope, you can walk your ass home with the baby. I don't care if you or the baby get sick and die." So, I had no choice. I quickly grabbed my baby, wrapped him up as well as I could in many blankets over his little head and body, and off I went to my house in the snow and sleet, and in my face, tears were warming up my cheeks and freezing almost instantly. I was praying with all of my heart that the baby and I would not get sick or die. This little man means everything to me, absolutely everything to me!

He's all I had at this point that I loved with everything in me, in that I know he would love me back. I got to the house; I quickly unwrapped him. He was okay; just a little bit cold. So, I pressed him up against me to warm him up and thank God he was fine. Nobody in my cousin's house could believe what just happened, but none of them had a car to take me home. They tried to convince him. He said he didn't care, not his problem. You're probably wondering if my decision was usual, right? The answer is yes, and for a week or two, he was sorry. He brought me flowers, and so our relationship continued.

Three or four weeks after my son Ernest was born, I went to high school and registered for classes. I was a freshman, but this was already the middle of February, so I missed a lot of material at this point. I remember the school shunning me and not wanting me to be in the class because of my condition— "a teen mother." They tried to convince me that it would be much better if I joined a teen mother program instead of going to high school. I think they feared that having a teenage mother in school was going to infect the other students.

I just couldn't do it! I didn't want to be a high school dropout; I didn't want to be another statistic—a young Hispanic teenage mother from the projects with no High school education, working a mediocre job for the rest of her life. I saw too much of that in the projects. I was already on my way to being a statistic, having a kid at 15 years old. The school was trying to stop me at all cost from attending. They told me if my grades were not good enough, that when school ended, I would have to join the teenage mother program. I would have to convince our town mayor and board of Education that I was worth taking a chance on. So, I fought! I needed to go to school. I absolutely needed to show my baby boy that just because things get tough, you don't quit. I refuse to have him also be a young Hispanic/Haitian boy that quits school and does nothing with his life. It was going to be tough enough that he was a minority. When I went to school, I remember the kids mumbling amongst themselves when I walked by, "Is that her? Is that the girl with a baby?" I would turn around in anger and embarrassment and tell them, 'Yes I am, mind your own business." I did pass all my classes, and I walked right up into the office of the mayor and slammed my grades on his desk and walked out. I was so damn proud of myself. It felt so good to do something right!

My home life started to get even more hard-hitting. I was working a job, going to school, being a mom, and fighting for my life all of the time. My son's father started to get more volatile, more aggressive, and more frightening. The arguments were almost every day and the beatings for almost daily. It was hard to breathe, to have a moment to myself to have any sort of peace. We were constantly breaking up, getting back together, having a day or two of happiness; you get the point! I was alone. I barely had friends because I was a mother and had to take care of my son, work, and go to school. The friends I had around the projects really liked my son's father and had no idea of the monster he was behind closed doors. The one friend I thought was a good friend turned out to be a whore who while I was pregnant, was giving my son's father sexual favors in the back seat of his car. With friends like that, who needs enemies?!

I got discouraged and didn't want any friends. I nearly beat her into the ground. Of course, he egged it on and wanted me to do it because he was angry that she told me. She was definitely not the first or the last girl he had on the side during our relationship.

As the months went on, my son's father started to get worse with his jealousy towards his son. He said to me, "If you pay more attention to him than me, while you're sleeping, I'm going to suffocate him." I said to him, "Are you crazy? That's your son?" He said, "Yes, I am crazy, and I was here first. So, I want the attention first!" At night, I would pull up a chair, sit next to my son's crib, and put my hand between the crib's bars, on his little chest and slept sitting down. I was absolutely terrified that if I fell asleep not next to my son, I would wake up to a dead child. I knew in my heart that this man was crazy enough to do it. I also conceded in my heart that if he did, I would be in jail for murder. As my baby started to grow up, I loved him more and more. I didn't think it was possible to love someone so darn much. My son's father did not like the fact that I love this little guy so much that I'd rather be with the baby than with him. About six weeks into having the baby, he couldn't wait anymore to have sex, so we got into a huge fistfight. He raped me, so of course, the stitches I had burst open, and I bled and was in pain for weeks. I felt so broken, used, and empty. It is a repulsive feeling to be beaten and forced upon against your will. I just laid there like a corpse, trying to block out what was happening and hoping it would repulse him and he would stop. He didn't, and when he was done, he had a smirk on his face and said, *it was good, right*? I just rolled over and cried. He used the F-word on me again and said I liked it. I felt terrible because I did this to myself; I deserved to be treated this way. I was too scared to leave.

I chose to move on from this and act like it never happened; he was my boyfriend anyway, so I just had to live with it. A few months went by and as I was attending high school and waiting for the school bus to come and pick me up so I can go to work. I had a girl approach me, asking me if

I am sleeping with a guy we all knew. I said no, what the hell are you talking about? She said, well, my best friend, Marybell, is dating him and she heard that you were sleeping with him. I said then call your best friend to ask me. So, Marybell came to talk to me, and she said people were telling her that I was trying to be with her boyfriend. I knew that was kids spreading rumors. They just wanted to see a fight, but I was not interested in him or in fighting. She happened to be the girlfriend of my son's father best friend. He was really the only person I talked to in the school; I wouldn't dare speak with another guy and girls didn't like me.

So, a few weeks after this encounter, she and I started talking after I sent her a letter, explaining that I had nothing to do with her boyfriend, but I was still with my son's father. That opened up the door of conversation, and before I knew it, she and I were inseparable and became best friends. She was a first-hand witness to a lot of the abuse and beatings from my son's father. She tried many times to convince me to leave, and I just was too terrified and too in love to go. My son's father was relentless; he also didn't like that I was friends with her because again, he was here first. My little Ernie loved her; we spent his first Christmas with her, and he took his first steps towards her.

Jealousy quickly became apparent, and because of this, our fights got intense. His solution was sex, and because I did not want to, he would beat and rape me. It was painful and demeaning; I felt so used and worthless. After a week or so, we made up. He appears so sorry, and this time, I could see it.

A few weeks later, Marybell and I were in the mall, shopping. My son's father was at the mall with his friends as well. They were teasing us as to why we were in the mall, who we were trying to look cute for. We, in turn, teased them and said we were up to no good. My son's father became extremely jealous of the teasing. It angered him how freely I was speaking to him in front of his friends, so he started calling me a whore and that I was his sloppy seconds and that no one would love me ever again, in front of his friends. His words became even uglier, so we started to leave, but he followed me and continued to verbally shout cruel sexual comments.

Finally, his friends pulled him away. After 10 minutes of Marybell trying to calm me down, I confessed to her that I thought I was pregnant again and that I was going to have his second baby. Marybell convinced me that we should leave the mall, but as we were leaving, he was waiting for us at the mall exit. He was angry, and I told Marybell to keep walking no matter what because I knew what was coming and I didn't want her to get hurt. Too late, he got in our way.

I went around him, and he pushed my head really hard twice, jerking it forward and kept trying to hurt me. I was saying just leave me alone. But he wouldn't leave me alone; it made him get worse. He picked me up and did a bear hug where he squeezed so hard he cracked my back, and I cried out, "NO, STOP, I MIGHT BE PREGNANT," and at that moment, he flipped me and turned me to the side and slammed my stomach against his knee. As I fell to the floor, he said NOT ANYMORE, you're not. By the time Marybell got the security mall officer, he had left. All I could do is cry in Marybell's lap in her car. Marybell said I need to leave him, but all I could say is that I love him and that I didn't understand why but I did, and I just didn't understand why he would hurt me so much. I just could not fathom the thought of giving this monster another child and having him torture that child or me for the rest of our lives. I was having a hard time protecting my Ernie as it was. I went to Planned

Parenthood and as much as I didn't want to. I felt like I had no choice and I got an abortion. It was so painful, emotionally and physically. I really felt so scared and alone. I tried going on different types of birth control, but they made me very sick.

Throughout the first couple of years, the beatings became stronger and more frightening. If I didn't want to, it was not an option—it was constant fighting and beatings. I did become pregnant two more times and had two more abortions. When I had the abortions, especially the last one, I didn't tell my son's father. I don't know how but he did find out, found me at the clinic and when I was leaving, he was standing at the door, spitting in my face, yelling at me that I was a murderer, a whore, a loser, and a bitch. Damn, I cried a lot over this and regretted it then and still do. I was just young and frightened for my life and the life of my child. I had all of these events and abortions, and I wasn't even 17 yet. I couldn't do it anymore! I had to find a way out.

He was beating me often in front of my baby boy. Ernie would jump in the way and scream to the top of his lungs, "Don't hit my mommy," "Stop hitting my mommy." He would just push my son to the side and punch me in the face or smack me; whatever he was in the mood for at the moment.

It would always be for silly things like if I beat him at a game playing Atari or Nintendo, if I didn't agree with a statement he said or if I question something about his whereabouts, etc. It didn't take much to set him off.

Believe it or not, he was a very persuasive and charismatic young man, not just to me but to my family and our friends, except for Marybell who couldn't stand him at all. She tolerated him because of me. Everybody thought I was exaggerating when I would tell them what he was doing

66

to me. You must be doing something to make him mad, they would say. Even my grandmother asked, *what are you doing to make him mad*? Everyone but Marybell agreed, he just doesn't seem like the type.

My mother was on his side, the mutual friends we had were on his side, some of his family members were on his side, all I had on my side was my best friend and my son. He would buy my mother gifts all of the time, like a microwave or a blender, a small TV, and she ate it up. This made him better than me because I didn't buy those things, that made me an ungrateful child...

In my mom's view, my son's father could do no wrong; he was a much better son to her than I was a daughter. For example, one day, when my son was about two years old, we went out with Marybell, and when she dropped me off at home, I went into the house, and as I was trying to close the door behind me, my son's father pushed the door open and followed me in. At this point in time, we had split up, so he was following me around as usual after a breakup. I asked him what he was doing at my place, and he said he knows that I've been whoring around. I told him to leave and get out. I said mom, tell him to get out, but he walked up to me and punched me in the center of my chest so hard that I literally had no air left in me to breathe. I fell to my knees and thought I was going to die. Talk about knocking the wind out of you. All of a sudden, Marybell ran into the house because while she was pulling off, she noticed him walking towards the house. She pushed him off, got on the floor with me, held me in her arms and I grabbed onto her. I looked up at my mother who was standing there watching the entire thing and when I could take a short breath; I said, "Mommy...call the cops." She said, "Nope, this is not my problem," grabbed her purse and walked out. So, Marybell yelled at him, grabbed the phone and called the cops, and he ran away. I was so frightened because it seems like there was no way out of this prison.

He was so scary when I wasn't with him. At least, when I was with him, I could try to control the situation, right? When we break up, it's a whole different type of demon that comes out.

There was one day he took my son for the weekend, and my son and him were outside of my mother's apartment. There was a guy on the block that wanted to talk to me on a personal level, and my son's father found out. We were broken up at this point, so I liked the guy. My son's father was following me as usual, and the boy was in my mom's home with me. We were making out, and I saw a shadow by the window; I immediately got scared and told him to leave because I think my son's father is here. It was a Sunday, he was there to drop off my son and I was terrified because I knew that he was going to hurt me. He had my son knock on the door and yell out: *mommy, it's me, open the door*. I said, *no sweetheart, I cannot open the door*, and I can hear his father whispering because I had my ear pressed up against the door. And he said to my boy again, *tell her to open the door*. So, my son repeated it. My heart was pounding so bad I could feel it in my throat. I said no sweetheart, I can't open the door right now. Then my son's father pounded on the door and said if you don't open the door, I will cut him right here! Oh my God, my baby, I have to open.

At that exact moment, my mother and my stepfather were walking into the house and asked what was going on. I told them that he threatened to hurt the baby and me. So, she turned around and asked again. He said nothing at first, and later said he was just bringing the baby back and 'your whore of a daughter had a boy in the house.' She took Ernie from

68

him while I stood in the back near the kitchen, absolutely terrified. He looked at me but didn't dare to come in; I almost peed in my pants.

My mother told me later that when she walked up, he was outside with a beer bottle broken in his hand. He told me later that he was going to cut my face up if I had opened that door. At this point, I was more determined not to go back to him because it started to get so bad.

There were times I would be sleeping with my baby on the bed, and I would wake up in the middle of the night, and he would be standing at the foot of my bed just staring at me. He would break the lock on the window and come right in. I would be so scared and tried acting unmoved, "What are you doing here?" He would say I'm making sure you're alone. He would just knock on the door, and my mom would just open it for him even though she knew what he was doing to me.

While we were still apart, Marybell, my mom, my little sister, and I were in my room. I was standing in my doorway when out of nowhere, my son's father came up the stairs with an angry energy, almost as if he was getting ready to do something. He would clench his fists. I turned to look at him, hoping to engage him in a conversation and determine how bad his mood was before anything happened. He wanted to take my son, so he came into my room and started packing the baby's bag, and I said NO, you can't take him! Before I could fully turn my face, he punched me with a closed fist so hard on my left side of my face, and the right side of my face bounced off the wall, and I slid to the floor. He stood over me and uttered *get up* repeatedly. My mom was saying you see, this is what you get! Marybell came over to see if I was okay, but I blacked out. When I became conscious, I called out to my mom for help, and she grabbed my little sister and

69

said this wasn't her business. When Marybell saw my mom wasn't calling the cops, and my son's father wasn't letting up, Marybell got around him, she ran downstairs, called the cops and yelled at him to leave me alone and said she has called the cops. Only then did he leave because he was still kicking and punching me until he heard the cops were coming.

When Marybell got to where I was upstairs, my ear was already bleeding, my right eye was bloodshot, and my face was swollen. When she called the cops, I decided to get a restraining order. Till this day, I have 60% equilibrium difference in my ears and a hole the size of the pinhead in my left ear where his hit was. I have definitely been close to death in this relationship. I have been punched in the face and body, had black eyes, thrown down the stairs, choked, raped, verbally abused, spit on, peed on, and nearly killed.

He apologized and pleaded, so I took him back because what would happen if I didn't take him back? Marybell kept pleading and telling me that I have to get away, that I can't keep living like this. It's not good for my son or me to continue to live with this guy. I knew that, but I just didn't know how to get out of it. I mean he would show up at my job, in my house, in my bedroom in the middle of the night, pop out from a car or behind a tree when I was walking somewhere. He was absolutely terrifying, scary, vicious, and demonic. What do I do? How do I get out and live?

I was constantly sitting with my thoughts; I would write lyrics to songs; it was my escape. Marybell and I would write original songs and sing them everywhere we went. At school, we would go to the court or the front of the school and start singing our songs; crowds would form around us and they would sing along. The songs were freestyle and popular at the time. They became "hits," and you would hear other kids just walking around the hallways of the high school singing our songs, like Marybell's song, "Going all the way" or my song, "You Broke my heart." I would hear them and ask where they heard the song. They would say, on the radio, I think. I felt so good about that. Then Marybell graduated and school stopped being so fun.

So, the following year, I decided that since our high schools first talent show was about to happen, I had to get prepared. I watched Jennifer Lopez and the dancers on *In Living Color* for some more dance moves and practiced with Marybell after school and made some up of my own. I was performing Lisa Lisa and Cult Jam, "Together Forever." Everyone said I reminded them of her, so I thought this could work. My son was always with me and Marybell, and so he knew all the dance moves and would practice with us, and if we forgot the moves, he would correct us. It was so much fun, and I loved having those moments of beauty in the middle of the mess. When the day came, my son was at my mom's, so I asked my son's father to bring him, and he said he would. I asked him to please help me buy the video so I could have it for the baby when he grows up; he said okay.

Then the day came, I was so nervous and excited; I couldn't wait for my son to see me on stage. When it was my turn, I went up and I killed it, at least, that's what it seemed like because I got a standing ovation. I looked around, and there is my son's father but no son. Damn it! He couldn't even do that for me!! I was so pissed. I came down after the event and asked where my baby was. He said home, that he had a slight fever and he wouldn't remember this anyway. You weren't that good! It was all right. Ugh, the frustration was real. Everyone was coming up to me and telling me I had the best performance, but now, I didn't believe them because

71

my son's father might be an asshole, but he tells the truth. Right?

Of course, I never was able to afford the tape either, so now I don't have the memory to share with my son. Then like a week after that performance, I decided I wanted to record the song I wrote, and when I spoke with some talent scouts in Stamford they liked my performance and they wanted to record me, but I couldn't do it because I knew he wouldn't let me, or give me any support and I had to work and go to school so I can care for my son.

While we were back together, he convinced me that this time, it would be different, and it was for a few months. The honeymoon periods were always so enjoyable and amazing; it gave me hope that this could work, that we could be a family and even though my mother was constantly trying to convince me that he and I should get married and I should quit school already and get another job, I just knew in my gut that it was not a good idea.

Then one day, on my last year of high school, I was coming off the bus, and there was always a nauseating moment right before I got home of not knowing what mood I was walking into. On this particular day, I got home a little late because the bus was late picking us up from school; he was pacing around upstairs in my bedroom and says, *where were you? Why are you late*? I sent my son downstairs, and said, I'm only late because the bus was late picking us up. He said no, I bet you were out sucking someone else. Then he said if I can't have you, nobody can have you. I can't take it anymore; I'm going to kill you, then the baby, then myself.

When he turned around to look at me, his eyes looked black. I've never seen him look at me like this before. I asked what he was talking about. How can I be out there doing that when I'm only 15 minutes late? What the hell is wrong with you? Then I see it…he takes out a gun, cocked it back to load it and says, if I can't have you, no one can. Oh shit, survival mode kicked in. I said, are you kidding me? I don't want to be with anyone else; I love you so much! I would never be with anyone else. I love you and only you. I pleaded for my life. I begged. I told him I loved him; he was pacing back and forth, and my heart was pounding. I thought, how am I going to get out of this? He then turns around and walks right up to me, puts the gun to my head. The metal was cold; my body went numb and I closed my eyes, thinking this is it. He pulls the trigger, my body shuddered, and the safety lock got jammed. He got mad and was trying to unjam it. I quickly grabbed him and started telling him I love him and why would he want to hurt his family, that he meant everything to me and he shouldn't be this way to his son and me. It took what felt like a lifetime, but I was able to take the gun from his hand as he calmed down. I was trembling the whole day, thinking about what I was going to do. I will not let him kill my son. As the day passed, I made him dinner, and he fell asleep. I took the gun and pointed it at him while he was sleeping and wanted to shoot him, but I looked at my son who was sleeping on the other side of the room, and all I can think of was that I would go to jail for life and my son will not have me around, and my mother will raise him. The thought of it shook me back to my senses. I took the gun to a friend of ours in the neighborhood who said, oh yeah, he asked to hold it because someone was messing with him. I said no; he tried to kill my son and me. He was shocked, "Are you kidding me? I'm sorry, I will not give him anything again."

The next morning, I acted as if nothing was wrong. Gave him a goodbye kiss, same with my baby, then I got on the bus to go to school, so they thought. Marybell met me,

73

and we waited for him to leave for work. I came home, grabbed my baby, put some clothes in the garbage bag and before my mother could notice, I ran for my life. For a few days, my friend and I were already doing an escape plan to the nearest shelter, and this was the opportunity, so I went to a shelter. We were rejected from the first shelter because they weren't for battered women. They referred me to another shelter and I went there. I was so scared, but I knew I had to do this. They were very kind to me and gave me a shared room with two other women. That night, my son was playing on the window sill with a matchbox car, and I narrated to the women what has happened to me. Suddenly, I hear my son say, "Hi daddy" and wave. "Mommy, daddy's outside." I grabbed him from the window and shut the light off in the room, and when I peeked out the screen, there he was, waving at me. The absolute nightmare comes to reality! I was so terrified I almost passed out! How the hell did he find me? Oh my God, what am I going to do? The women who were in the room with me said they wouldn't say anything, but if he tries to get in here, they are going to kick me out because no one is supposed to know this is a battered women's shelter. After he drove away, I called my mom that evening and told her that I was okay and that the baby was okay. She said I'll pay for leaving and taking the baby. I said mom, he put a gun to my head and pulled the trigger and said he was going to kill me, the baby and himself. She said *yeah, he should've done it; you're going to regret taking the baby; you'll see.* I said to her, mom, did you tell him where I was? She said *yes, that's right. I found the pamphlet that you had, and I told him where you were; good he found you.* I said, *mom, he's going to kill me.* She said, *well, after this stunt, you deserve it.* I hung up the phone in complete disbelief of what I just heard. He actually brought her favor with a few appliances. She went against her own daughter's life and her grandson's life so she can continue to have gifts, money, and the power over us to control our lives. Not to mention that just a few weeks before she said to me: *don't bother fixing up this room much because you're going to be leaving soon. My daughter needs her own room, and you're taking up the space here.* I asked her, *where am I going to go with a baby?* She replied, *I don't know, that's not my problem.*

So, now what? What am I going to do now? He knows where I am, he knows where my son is, and I have to continue going to school and work. This was my last year of high school, and failure is not permissible. I have to graduate even if it's just with the bare necessities to graduate. I cannot quit! I can't let my son see me quit. What am I going to do? All I can think of is I'm going to have to play it off and play nice with my son's father. Lie to him and tell him that my mom wanted me out of the house. Because if I don't, he's going to break windows and cause havoc and get me kicked out of the only place I have to live. I knew he would follow me to school, follow me to my son's daycare, follow me to work, follow me to the store, and everywhere I go. I could only dodge him for a little bit, then here we are face-to-face as I came out of class walking towards my bus. He waited outside, leaning on his car between the school and my bus. I was freaking out! I knew what was coming; I had to get to my bus. I started walking as quickly as I can towards the bus, and he ran up to me and grabbed me by my hair, kicking me and people were watching, but I fought him off and thought, I just have to get to the bus. I start picking up the pace and running. I made it to the bus and the bus driver was like, get in, just get in. I made it on the bus, and he just followed the bus. Everyone was asking me if I was okay. I said yes, he's just an asshole. At this point, Marybell, my only best friend had already graduated, so I was in school by myself. It was more of an opportunity for him to torture me right after school.

In the shelter, they made sure that they help with whatever they could. They helped my son get into the daycare not too far from the shelter. They also helped me find a sitter when I was done with school. Before then, I would take the bus from school, go pick up my son, drop him off at the babysitter and then go to work at the supermarket as a cashier on some days and at JC Penny's on other days. I walked everywhere I had to go, picking up and dropping off my son, shopping for groceries, taking him to the doctors (whatever had to get done). My son's father kept showing up almost every day. So finally, I said okay, I'll meet with you, and I went outside, got in his car and was absolutely praying that he wouldn't kill me. At this point, he didn't even seem angry anymore; he looked more hurt that I left him. I told him I can't live like this anymore; it's just too much and I have to finish school. I have to take the baby to daycare and I have to work. He said okay, he understood and that he is sorry about what he did, and that he just loves me so much that it drives him crazy. I told him I love him too, but we need a break. He didn't like that suggestion very much. I can see his temples throbbing, and I knew that he was about to get explosive. So, I quickly excused myself and told him I'd see him soon. Surprisingly, he said okay and that he will not cause a scene at the shelter. I told him good because if you do, they will move us all the way up to Waterbury. He didn't want that, so he kept his composure.

I was at the shelter for close to a year, and while I was there, I decided I needed to find some family. I started asking my mother questions about any family or people that she can remember that I can contact to see if I have siblings from my

76

dad's side. My mom told me about a woman she remembers that lived in Norwalk but I would have to look up the white pages and call everyone with my biological father's last name—Robles. My name was not that since he never claimed me, but everyone knew I was his. There was no denying that. So, I picked up the white pages and started dialing the first name I saw. I left a message stating my name and that my father's name is Paul and that I just want to know if I have a family out there. I was lonely, scared and tired of feeling unwanted. I felt like I have to belong somewhere. Then one day, my manager at JC Penney's had me doing the credit card applications at the front of the store for new customers, and my supervisor comes up to me and says, *hey, someone's looking for you.* I instantly froze because I thought it was my son's father. Then I looked up, and this guy was standing there, and he said, *hey, I hear you are looking for some family?* I'm your brother Paul,

What?!!! Just like my father! I dropped all the applications I had in my hand and ran to him and hugged him and started crying. I couldn't believe it!!! A connection to my dad's side of the family. He confirms who he is and that he would like me to meet his mom and my other brother. I was so excited!! I gave him my number at the shelter because it was the only way I could be reached. A few days later, he picked me up and took me to his mom's house in Norwalk. He sits me down and says, *Sis, are you living in a shelter?* I asked, *how do you know that that's confidential?* He said, *I asked the girl that picked up the phone, and she told me.* I was so embarrassed. The place is supposed to be confidential; I wanted to 'kill' her for telling him. I looked to the ground and said, *yes, it's a battered women's shelter.* He immediately became concerned and said, "What!? Who is he? You have a big brother now; I will kick his ass if he

77

touches you." Whoa!!! Freaking cool! I loved the way that felt!!! I said wow, really and started tearing up. He gave me a big hug and said, *do you still talk to this dude*? I said, "Yes, I'm afraid not to." He said, "Okay. Bring him here, tell him your brothers want to meet him." I know what you're thinking…did I do it? Well then, of course, I had to do it!! I told him I wanted him to meet my other side of the family. He thought that was great. He came with me to Norwalk, and my brother Paul asked, *is this him*? I said yes, and he yoked him up and said, *if I find out that you ever dare to lay a finger on my little sister again, I will kill you and no one will find you. She's not alone anymore. Do you understand*? He said yes! My brother let him go, and my son's father looked at me with frustration, but I just grinned and loved every second of it. Then my brother sent him on his way and said, *you can go, I will take her home*. Ahhhhh, beauty in the middle of the mess!!!

The next day, my son's father came to talk to me and said, *why in the f**k did you do that*? I told him, I just wanted you to understand that I am not alone anymore. I will have no hesitation calling my brothers. He didn't like that and looked like he wanted to hit me, so I dared him! He didn't, and I felt empowered.

Shortly after, my time at the shelter ran its course and my aunt had a room. She could rent me a room upstairs in her home, so I took it. I worked, took care of my baby and now, I had to get on some state assistance because I couldn't afford to pay the room rent and still feed and clothe my son let alone myself. I hated living on state assistance, even though I always knew it was for help and it was temporal, but I just didn't want to be like my mother living off the system all my life. I hated that now I was really looking like a statistic. I graduated high school by the skin of my teeth. An 18-year-

78

old with a three-year-old son, on state assistance, WIC, working a low-level paying job at JC Penney's and now renting a room just to try and make it. I had no plans nor confidence to go to college. I was beaten down so much about how stupid I was. I just didn't think I could do it and besides, who would take care of my son?

When I was about 19 years old, I got the brilliant idea that I would join the army and become a military police officer; I wanted to be disciplined. I wanted to know how to fight the right way; I wanted me and my son to escape his father, and I wanted my son to be proud of me. So, I signed up, took some exam and when I was at the office talking to them about swearing in, the recruiter says, "Wait, you have a son?" I said yes, and he said that I had to give up custody of my son. No freaking way I'm doing that. He said, "Ma'am, you could leave it with your mother or his father." Is he crazy, hell no!!!! So, instead, I started dating the recruiter, the closest thing I got to joining the army. He was much older than I, so nothing serious ever came out of it and sadly, I don't remember his name. I was trying to escape and move on from my messed-up relationship with my son's father. There has to be something better.

My son's father was now coming around my aunt's house, asking me out and trying to buy me things. When I didn't yield, it was the pulling of the hair and squeezing my arms so tight he would leave terrible bruises. I would yield sometimes and be with him because I was terrified he would cause damage to my aunt's house and I didn't want her to be mad at me and kick me out. He would follow me everywhere. There was a moment I was at my friend's house, and we were going for a walk in her nice neighborhood, just me, her and my baby boy. All of a sudden, he comes out from behind a tree, my girlfriend says, "Run Neena, run." So,

79

I started running with my son. He grabbed our son and took him. He put him in the car and yelled out the car window: *I'm going to take him to Haiti, and you will never see him again.* I started screaming, OH MY GOD! OH MY GOD! HELP, HELP! I can't describe to you the fear and pain that came over me. I started shaking in fear. I knew him well enough to know that he was not kidding. We quickly ran into her house, and I called the cops. I told them everything, and they told me he had the rights to take him because I didn't have sole custody. I told them I need them to get my son because he's going to take him to his family's home in Haiti and I will never see my son again. After a few minutes of explaining the domestic violence, the cop felt bad for me and said, *okay, we will see what we can do.* I told them to look at his mother's house first. They went to his mother's house and found my son. They told him that he couldn't take the kid like that or he can be charged with kidnapping, so they took my son and brought him to me and said, you better go to the courts ASAP and get this matter fixed, or you will not have any chance of taking your son back if this ever happens again.

Of course, I immediately went to the courthouse and filed the paperwork. That caused a rage in my son's father that was unquenchable. He was more aggressively following me, walking up to me and getting close to my ear to curse me out, pushing me hard to the ground when he had the chance, but I didn't care. He wasn't taking my son! We went to court, while I was waiting for my pro-bono lawyer to come to the court, my son's father sat next to me on the bench and was whispering in my ear, calling me bitch, whore, prostitute and that he is going to beat the shit out of me as soon as we went outside for making him go through this and that he will contest and fight me for custody, and he would win because I

80

was such a loser and a bad mother. I was scared, and my stomach hurt from the nerves, but I still didn't care; he wasn't taking my son.

All I kept thinking was that if he takes my son, I am going to literally kill him and run away with my son, but he's not taking my son. When both of the lawyers arrived, I couldn't believe he actually went out and got a lawyer. We were in a mediation room, and my son's father says, I want to fight her for full custody; she's a bad mother. I stayed quiet; I leaned over to my lawyer and said he was just trying to intimidate me right outside the room before we started. His lawyer proceeded to say that my son's father had a good job, was a responsible father and he had the right to fight for his son's custody. My son's father says yes, that's right, I'm a good father and I want my son to live with me, and she can have visitation rights. So, my lawyer said, "Really? You're a good father?" And proceeded to unfold a very long list that actually hit the floor when he unfolded it, of all the restraining orders, arrests for domestic violence and disturbing the peace.

That document was vital in having everything go in my favor to take and keep sole custody of my son. The court ordered for me to have sole custody of our son and for him to have visitation rights and for him to pay $45 a week in child support. That ruling was on March 1, 1993; my little man was five years old and everything I had to live for. He was absolutely every reason I had to breathe and fight back. During all of this high stress, I quickly became a bit of a wild child. Marybell and I started going to clubs, smoking cigarettes, drinking when we went out, smoking weed and joining dance competitions at different clubs around Connecticut/NY. Cigarettes were more my thing; I didn't like weed. It made me paranoid, so I stopped that pretty quickly.

81

We practiced a lot of our dance moves and we were damn good and always won free prizes, entry tickets, etc. I would leave my son with my mom, who even though she didn't give a crap about me, loved my son to bits.

Finally, my son's father started dating a girl named Tanisha. It wasn't unusual for him to sleep around behind my back but I heard that he liked her a lot more than the other ones, and I noticed he wasn't coming around as much. One day, I bumped into this girl I heard about in the Stamford mall as Marybell and I were hanging out. She was very pretty; I could see why he liked this one. She already knew who I was. I called her over, and she looked terrified and skeptical. I think she thought I was about to start a fight. I said, "Are you his new girlfriend?" She said "yes," and backed up a little bit. I leaned in and I said, "THANK YOU!" Everyone around us was shocked. I think they thought they were going to witness a cat fight. I think if I could kiss and hug her, I would have. "Please, keep him happy! Please keep him busy." I want him to leave me alone, so I appreciate it. She just looked at me perplexed and said *oookkkkie*. I was hoping I didn't scare her off; she was my way out of this nightmare. I was FREE! I was FREE! He likes someone else.

Lord, thank you; please, let it go really well. I kind of felt bad for her, but I was really selfish and didn't care as long as my son and I would find some peace. As time passed, she and I had a respectful relationship because my son had to have visitation with his father. I like her very much till this day. She was kind to my son, always willing to pick him up and spend time with him even when his father wasn't around. She is pretty and very smart and kind. She and my son's father were having a great relationship from what I can tell, and I was happy for her. One day, she told me she was pregnant and I felt an overwhelming fear come over me for

82

her because that's when he became even more evil with me. I told her some of the stories and told her to please be careful. Well, they had a child together, and sure enough, he started changing and shortly after, she had her daughter. He hit her one time and she was out! She was smarter and stronger than I was. He started to do the same things to her, where he would be hiding in closets, etc. She wasted little time; she left the state with her daughter…SMART!

Now, Marybell and I, who is my partner in crime, were unstoppable. I started dating other guys, to try and forget my son's father and his crazy ass abuse. I started street racing, and that was a lot of fun, and quickly, I became an adrenaline junkie. I loved weaving around cars, racing through town and challenging cars on the street. We used to go to Norwalk, Bridgeport, Bronx, Queens, Brooklyn. It was crazy to feel this sense of freedom, meeting new people, and experiencing new things. I swear Marybell was sent to me from heaven to help me through the years of hell. She witnessed so many beatings, she called the cops, she would help me by letting my baby and I stay at her house, even though she was going through her own hell with her boyfriend. We supported each other through so many storms. She also brought me my 18th birthday cake after so many years of not getting one. She is still my dearest friend today; it's nearly 30 years.

While I was feeling this sense of freedom my son's father was still coming around to instill some fear but it was far less frequent, and I was done being scared. I now just loathed him. I couldn't stand his presence. I started going out more, so I was less at home, and therefore, less of a chance of having to deal with that idiot.

On one of our adventures to the clubs I met a really handsome young man, caramel skin, hazel contacts, dark

curly short hair, reminded me of my favorite rapper, L.L.
Cool J... yep, I'm going in. This guy was fun, funny,
handsome and from NY so he will not know about my son's
father and all the crap everyone around town knew about the
abuse and all I've been through.

He and I quickly became inseparable, we were
hanging out with his friends in Armonk NY, Yonkers, and
White Plains. His life seemed pretty interesting. He told me
he was a twin but his mom kept him and his father took his
brother. His father supposedly was a big-time drug dealer in
NY and he didn't want anything to do with him. He told me
how he was loyal to his mother and his stepbrother who he
grew up with. Listening to these stories made me question if
he was telling the truth but hey, why would he lie, I don't
know him from a can of paint.

Listening to all the stories he told was fun and out of
my dramatic, dark and overwhelming hectic life. Of course, it
wasn't long when my son's father found out that I was
dating, and one day when my new man was at my aunt's
house to pick me up, out of the darkness comes my son's
father with his friends to try and jump my new boyfriend. I
told my aunt to call the cops and my son's father ran back to
his car with his friends and they took off.

Chapter 3

THE NEW BOYFRIEND!

Right after that crazy night, my new boyfriend of just a few months told me that he's not leaving me in CT alone with that crazy person. That was so sexy and so good to hear. He told me he had fallen in love with me and he didn't trust him, and he wanted to protect my son and me. I wasn't really in love with him, but there was a very strong chemistry that could grow into love. I'm 19 turning 20 years old, and I was tired of fighting so much and doing it alone. He asked me to grab some of my things from my aunt's house and come to be with him for the weekend at his mother's house in Yonkers. Of course, I couldn't resist a chance to meet his family, especially his mom. My son and I went there for long weekends often to escape our chaos and to get to know the family. We got along great with his family; they were very receptive and kind to my son. We had time to go because I just got fired from JC Penney's for being late because I never seemed to master balancing my time to take the city bus to my mother's across town to drop off my son and then walk like 1 ½ -2 miles to work. I never had enough money for anything extra like a cab.

My aunt was not having it with me being short or late on rent and I knew there was no mercy there, so I had to figure out my next steps to make it through. I would take others' leftovers home to eat so my rent could get paid. Thank God for welfare in time of need, WIC program, and food stamps. When those came at the beginning of the month, we felt rich because there was food. My son loved his cereal like Cornflakes with sugar added; our version of frosted flakes, Trix, Kix, Sugar Crisp, Froot Loops, and Fruity Pebble. Ernie loved tearing the boxes to get the prizes in the bottom of the box. He also loved fruit roll-ups, cracker jacks and fruit of any kind. I used to have a little hot plate and some cheap cookware I brought from Woolworth. I would call it "cooking" when I made Rice a Roni with a side of can corn with some butter and salt, Spaghetti-o's, Beefaroni, Velveeta mac and cheese from the box and add ground beef and Hamburger Helper. When I didn't want to "cook," I would buy him the frozen TV dinners called Kid Cuisine. It was what I could make on a hot plate or small microwave, and what I could afford. Some of the things would actually be like two for a dollar; can't beat that when you're on a budget! Although I still loved and wished I was a cook like Julia, I had bigger fish to fry.

It wasn't long before I couldn't afford to pay my aunt anymore now that I lost my job. I refuse to live on welfare like everyone else I knew. I kept looking for work. It just so happened as I was staying with my boyfriend at his mother's house, his cousin had a family emergency. Her mother was ill and possibly dying in Puerto Rico, so she asked if I could fill in for her at her doctor's office in Yonkers since I wasn't working. I have never worked in a doctor's office before, so I wasn't sure I could do it. She told me she would train me and the doctor would be willing to have me fill in until she gets back which she figured would be like a month. So, I agreed to help. My boyfriend spoke to his mother and they agreed that I could move in until we get our own place. I really didn't feel like I had anything to lose and I would be far away from the drama and have my son with me.

The first day at the doctor's office was intimidating. I had to buy a white nursing uniform and a stethoscope. She introduced me to everyone, the doctor and the front of house receptionist, an extremely long and thin man named Billy. I was super nervous. I only worked at supermarkets, fast food and retail—this was a whole different ballgame.

First thing was triaging the patients, asking for their history and reason for the visit. Once she did that, she taught me how to take the height and weight, blood pressure, and temperature. Woah, working with people at that intimate level made me feel like I was imposing on their business. As the day progressed, she showed me how to set patients up for GYN exams, take an EKG for their hearts during their physicals, urine analysis and spirometry for the breathing exams. The last thing she showed me for the day was to take blood. TAKE BLOOD! Is she nuts?!

Okay, she says you need to have everything ready when you get the laboratory form from the doctor that tells you what he wants to be done for the patient. The test will tell you on the side what tubes you need. You need to look at the patient's arms and tie the tourniquet on that arm to find a vein you think would be good to take blood out of. She showed me the necessary equipment and how to use them like blood collection tubes, gloves, an assortment of needles and syringes of different sizes, alcohol swabs to clean the area to poke, gauze or cotton balls, laboratory forms, and blood specimen labels, transportation bags, etc. I looked at her like she was on crack when she said I should go for it, that I can do it, and she will let me attend to the next patient.

Oh, my goodness! I was sick to my stomach. The next patient came in with the form, and the beads of sweat on my forehead felt so big you can drown in them. She announces to the patient: *Okay ma'am; Neena is going to take your blood now.* I looked at the woman's arms, and they were so scarred up I couldn't see anything. I put on the tourniquet and started feeling around for something to pop up. Finally, it did pop

87

up, and I grabbed the needle that was attached to the tube and I was shaking so bad that everyone could visually see it. The patient said, "Don't worry about it, it's super easy, and I'm used to using needles so it won't hurt me at all." I took a deep breath and in I went; I got it! First try, and I got it. I couldn't believe I was able to pull that off. After that, she kept having me do the blood of other patients and would help me if I had difficulty getting it. She only trained me for a couple of days; I was on my own after that. The doctor was nice enough because he knew that I was just being helpful and that I didn't really have any experience doing this. It was exciting to be working again and was super exciting to be doing something new and different. Within a few weeks, I felt like I had the hang of this and had been doing it for a year. This doctor was always jam-packed, and the majority of his patients consisted of minorities, lots of HIV positive needle-using drug users and the mentally impaired. They were a very difficult group of people to work with because they were always high, aggressive, impatient, and very demanding.

I would always check on Billy because he had to deal with the patients first before me or the doctor got to see them. Billy and I started to get along very well. He would always say he's Jewish but wants to be Hispanic, so he learned Spanish and spoke it better than me. He was so tall, maybe 6' 3", super thin and a very kind human being. He would tell me about his "gay escapades" as he would call them and how many men he's been with. He told me he was also HIV positive and was a patient of the doctors and that's how he got the job. He was gang-raped in a park in NY city one day on his way home from an event, and that's how he contracted HIV.

I adored Billy; he was so interesting and fun to be around. I hated the way the doctor we worked for treated him, but I wasn't really an employee and didn't want to get my boyfriend's cousin in trouble for speaking my mind, so I would just tell Billy to speak up for himself, that he didn't deserve to be discriminated against. Billy was afraid of the doctor and also terrified of losing the little money he was making. Back then, HIV was a death sentence, and he knew that no one else would hire him if they knew about his condition.

After working with the doctor for a month, I took it upon myself to organize the office, the patient files, the lab forms, the confidential paperwork, the cabinets with the doctor's tools and so much more. The doctor was so impressed with my work ethic that when my boyfriend's cousin came back to the States, he told her he wanted to keep me. She agreed because she didn't want to come back to work. So now, I live in Yonkers and have a job. My little Ernie got registered for school, and we were living with my boyfriend's parents, not ideal, but my boyfriend was also working so we can get out ASAP.

Finally, after a few months, we saved up enough to get our own apartment. Ernie had his own room, a little TV and his own video game system and lots of games to go with it. I felt like I was moving up in the world. School for me was still out of the question, but now, I had a decent job, an apartment and an ugly doo-doo brown Dotson I think it was. That car was so bad we used to have to pour hot water over the engine in the winter time to get it started. My boyfriend would normally take the car and Ernie to school because they had to leave before me. I would take the city bus which was just fine with me.

Ernie was having a hard time not sleeping with me in the bed. I felt bad, but I had to break him out of the habit. He would only be allowed to sleep with me when our heat got cut off from Yankee gas for late payment. My little man would always show up around one in the morning saying, *mommy, I'm scared*, and I would either scoot over for him to climb in or I would go to his room and get him back in his bed. After a few months, he finally started sleeping alone in his room. How I wish I had those moments back!

One day, on my way to the city bus stop, I wasn't feeling well, and I got dizzy. I made it to the bus stop and started throwing up in the city garbage can. I don't know why, but I know I'm not pregnant. I have my period and have been bleeding for like 14 days at this point and didn't understand why this was happening, and I've been on a birth control pill for going on two years, now that I found one that doesn't make me sick. All I kept thinking is, I hope this pill isn't making me sick now like the rest of them.

When I got to work, out of curiosity, I took a urine pregnancy test, and the damn thing came out pink with two lines!!! Say what now?! Not possible, I am bleeding as we speak, I am faithful in taking my pills, so something is wrong. I took a tourniquet, tied it around my arm and took my own blood to see if I was really pregnant. Three days later, YEP, congratulations, I'm pregnant. I couldn't believe what I was reading on the paper, so I made Billy read it as well just to make sure I wasn't losing it. I called my boyfriend to come to my job and had him sit down so I can tell him. When I told him, he was so excited. He got up, hugged me, and all I kept thinking is, *oh my God, what am I going to do with another baby? Can I do this? Will I be able to love it as much as I love my Ernie? Is the baby going to be okay?* I've been taking my pills, smoking cigarettes, had a

90

drink or two in the last few weeks, oh my goodness, my poor baby. Why am I still bleeding? This makes no sense. I told the doctor and he sent me for an ultrasound. It turned out that there was an empty sac next to the baby's sac. Was there another baby that I might have miscarried and that's why I was bleeding for so long? Was it just an empty sac? No one had an answer. All I knew is that I was going to be super careful and take care of this pregnancy at all costs. My boyfriend was super sweet, always getting things for me, so I didn't lift things, running to the store if I had a craving and keeping Ernie busy if I had things to do. This pregnancy was such a different experience than Ernie's, at least this boyfriend seemed to give a crap most of the time. We still had some nasty arguments, but he never raised a hand to me. I don't think he dared because I warned him that the next person to raise a hand to me would surely die a vicious death. Although I knew in my heart that wasn't true; I sounded very convincing.

After a couple of months of the pregnancy, my boyfriend took Ernie out for a bit to let me rest. While I was sleeping, he and Ernie went downtown Yonkers shopping. When they got home, my boyfriend says, *hey, I got something for you, sit up.* So, I got up, sat on the couch, and he gave me the 10-gallon empty fish tank. He says I know you wanted a fish tank, so here you go. I said *aww, thank you.* He says now, look inside. When I look in, I saw a small box. I said what's this, and he gets on one knee and opens the box and says, *I love you very much, and I want our baby to be born while we are married, will you marry me?* Pause...I immediately started thinking, should I do this? I mean I love him but I don't love him like that. I've caught him lying a few times. I don't know if I fully trust him; he throws tantrums for no reason, and he calls his mommy to come to the house every time we fight like a child. I mean he's good to my son and he doesn't hit me. It would be nice to have my kids have a real…then he interrupts…hello, I asked you a question. I said *oh, yes of course, yes*. He puts the ring on my finger, probably one of the smallest diamonds I've seen but we didn't have much, and it was a sweet gesture. I hugged him and thought, *shit, what did I just do!?* My Ernie comes running in saying *yay, my mommy is getting married* and hugs me. I'm sure he was so happy to be away from all the drama and abuse he saw towards me. Plus, he was starting to love my boyfriend, so win-win, right?

A few months go by; we planned an extremely small wedding with the justice of the peace, then a family gathering in the small apartment we were renting. My mom came and said, *well, it's about time, this time you did it right*. It irritated me that she always has something to say but at least, she said something somewhat "nice," and it did feel good to get married to someone who was better than the last piece of garbage I was with.

My pregnancy was so hard on all of us. I was constantly having false alarms because the baby was so low that you could practically feel his head. We were constantly going to the OB/GYN office to check the baby and the heart rate. My Ernie was so sick of going back and forth, so he said to me, *mommy, the baby is taking so long, he's going to be like two years old when he comes out*. Oh, my goodness, I couldn't stop laughing. It must feel like an eternity when you're little and you're waiting like nine months. We didn't want to find out what sex the baby was so we could all be surprised. I was on bed rest the last three months because the baby was dangerously low and they were afraid I would have it on my way to work. I gained lots of weight; I was grumpy and getting depressed because I was home so much.

Then on January 27, 1994, on Ernie's 6th birthday, we brought him the Atari Jaguar with all the new released games like Chupa Chupa, Zool 2, Ultra-vortex and a few more. He was so excited. It was snowing outside and icy, so we just had us three at home, food, and a little cake. He thanked me and asked if we really know what he wants for his birthday. We said okay, what? He says a baby brother. I said, okay babe, we will see; maybe God will give you a baby brother. So, that night, we set up his game, let him play a little longer because the weather was so bad outside. It was a Thursday. I didn't anticipate there would be any school the next day. After everyone was asleep, I felt something wet. I rolled over and said, "Honey, this time, it's for real; my water broke." He was shocked! Popped out of bed and started running around the house trying to get everything we needed. I was laying down; he got Ernest up and ready. He took the bag, the keys to the car, and I said, *hi there, I think you forgot one thing, me.* He asked, *are you okay?* I yelled: yeah, as my first contraction kicks in at that moment. He says, yep this is it! It was 3 AM, and it was so bad outside, slippery, and cold. I said okay, Ernie, we are going to take you to grandma's because your baby brother or sister is coming. He said, *no sister; I want a baby brother.*

We got to the birthing clinic and contractions were fast and strong. We had decided to have our baby with midwives. I also opted to have the baby in the Jacuzzi because it was supposedly helpful with the contractions. Well, it didn't feel any better; I was moaning in pain. The Dr. looks at me and says, *what's your problem, what are you moaning about?* I looked at her and said *because I'm in f**king pain, why do you think I'm moaning?* Well, it didn't take long, and it was time to push. I started pushing and pushing, and the baby's head comes out and rips me open

93

because they didn't believe in cutting a little bit to help the head. I instinctively close my legs, and my Dr. midwife punches my legs open, I take a deep breath. I grabbed my husband by the head and nearly drown him as I'm pushing. The baby comes out; they grab it out of the water, and I put it over my shoulder. She pinches it and nothing. I flip the baby forward and look below; yes, it's a boy. I put him back on my shoulder, and they spank him and nothing. He's not breathing. I quickly rub his back; the Dr. is spanking him again and nothing. I hold him tight and pray, *Lord God, please don't take my son, please God, don't take my son.* Then I heard a faint cry, so low no one heard it but me, then I hear it again. Oh my God, he's breathing. They have my husband cut the umbilical cord, and they take him immediately to another room. My husband and I looked at each other in terror. I say, go and check on him, see if he's okay. He didn't want to leave my side, but I made him go. My heart is pounding, and suddenly, I heard a loud cry. My heart leaped with joy; my baby boy is crying; he's alive.

The Dr. comes into the room and they take me to the place where we will be for the next few hours. As I lay there, the pediatrician we chose, whose office was upstairs, came down and said something is wrong with the baby's heart, that it's irregular. My husband looks at me, and you can see the fear in his face. At the same time, I feel this gushing of water coming out of me, so I called the Dr. over and asked if I am still supposed to be having water coming out. She replies in the negative and checked. She pulls the sheet over my knees and makes me scoot to the end of the bed, her eyes widen and she calls the other midwife over, whispers in her ear and the midwife runs out of the room. I say to her, *what's going on?* She says, *you're hemorrhaging.* There is a lot of blood coming out; it's not water. The midwife comes back with an injection to give me so that my uterus can contract. My Dr. presses hard against my stomach, and I feel a large mass come out. It was a huge blood clot, the size of a baseball splatters against her Dr.'s uniform. She turns pale. She says okay, give her the injection, but every time the midwife stuck in the needle, she would retract blood and had to find another spot to do it. Then another injection, then she presses again, and another huge blood clot comes shooting out. I started to feel very sleepy, so I told my husband that I feel really sleepy. The Dr. instructs him not to let me go to sleep, to keep me awake. She tells me to push, but I have zero energy; I just want to go to sleep.

My husband looks at me in complete fear; he feels like he's about to lose his baby and his wife at the same time. He holds my hand and says, *I can't lose you; I can't survive without you. If God has to make me choose, I choose you.* I said absolutely not; I choose the baby, he must live and he needs you and so does Ernie. I knew he loved that baby, but he was beside himself in fear. I prayed to God, please, if one of us must go, take me and not the baby. Please, don't take the baby. After a few more clots came out, I stopped pouring out blood significantly, and my uterus started contracting again. The injections started working, and the Dr. sowed me up. She was scared I might have lost too much blood, so she let me rest and tested my hemoglobin. It was really low but not necessary to have a blood transfusion. My son was doing well. The Dr. spanked him really hard, and he screamed to the top of his lungs which corrected the irregular heartbeat.

My husband held him in his arms and called him Justin. The name I chose, it was such a tender moment. I was so happy that this was different from the last pregnancy and birth. I just wanted the best for my boys. Baby Justin and I started resting and doing fine. My husband's mother came with Ernie and a few gifts. Ernie was so excited when he saw that his birthday wish came true and he had a little brother, born the morning after his birthday. We sat him down and handed him his little brother; he was so stoked to be holding him. I was thinking at that moment, how is it possible to feel this much intense love? I love my Ernie so much; I was afraid I couldn't love another child that much and yet when Justin was born, my love just duplicated with the same fervor and intensity. I was now a mom of the most wonderful little creatures ever created! Then, 4-5 hours later, we were released to go home. It's what we signed up for when we decided to do this midwife program the hospital was offering. The baby and I were exhausted; the baby had a huge lump on his head because when I closed my legs on his head, I caused a bruise which became like a blood collection under the skin that took months to dissipate. When he came home that day, he slept like 12 hours straight. I thought something was wrong, but he seemed fine. I lost so much blood; I was forced to stay in bed. The midwives were going to call me that evening and visit the next day to make sure all was well. They were trying to help me with breastfeeding, but the baby wasn't getting enough milk. For whatever reason, I just wasn't producing enough milk. We tried for about a month then finally, I went against the midwife's rules, and I had to resort to a bottle of formula. The baby literally drank two 4 oz. bottles back to back; he was starving. They weren't happy about it, but I didn't care. I only had four weeks of maternity leave, so I had to do this ASAP. He was a chunky monkey. He was 8lbs 11 ½ oz. and 21" long. Well, four weeks went by very quickly. I was back to work at the Doctor's office, but I was miserable.

I wanted to be home with the boys. As this little guy started growing, I noticed he did things at a faster pace than his older brother. He saw his brother walking, and he always wanted to be with him, so he would craw fast and one day, just got on all fours, started wobbling and then just ran. I couldn't believe my eyes; he was like eight months old and didn't even start by walking. He just wanted to run after his brother, so he did. He started talking a lot and singing all the time because that was me and Ernie's thing, singing all the time. It was so cute to hear him chiming in with us.

Being back at work was hard because the Doctor treating Billy so poorly was really getting to me. I told Billy to ask for a raise; he shouldn't be doing so much for so little. So, he took a deep breath, went into the Doctor's office and asked for his raise. The next day, the Doctor came in with a chair pillow and said, *Billy, here's your raise, sit on it, and it will raise you up*. I couldn't believe it, what an insult. I followed the Doctor. into his room, shut the door and told him that was a real asshole move he just did. That it is so wrong and it shows he has no mercy for a man who could be dying because of his condition. He looked at me and said, *I'm your boss, don't talk to me that way*. I just looked at him and wanted to explode, but I walked out of the office, knowing I could lose my job and won't be able to help contribute to the household. A few weeks later, Billy became very ill and was hospitalized. I went to see him and was so hurt because Billy was so tall he would only fit on the bed in a fetal position. He was so thin and frail. He looks at me and says, *you are a good friend, can you do me a favor*? I replied, *anything for you Billy*.

He says*, please go to my apartment and get my turtles. I have seven of them, they are babies, and they sleep with me at night; they must be scared I haven't been home*. I said, *of course, I'll watch them for you until you come home. Okay*, he said, *can you also make me a Puerto Rican dinner*

97

of rice and beans and pernil (roasted pork shoulder). I said
absolutely. I told him I would be back in a couple of days
with his dinner and I will go get the turtles right away. So,
my husband took me to his home in the city; we got his seven
red-eared turtles and their tank and brought them home to
take care of. Ernie was excited to have animals in the house.

So, on that Wednesday, I went home straight from
work to make the dinner for Billy, and my husband had
cleaned the house and had made dinner for us. He says, *hey,
can you sit for a minute?* I said sure, but it has to be short
because I need to make this dinner for Billy. He says, *babe,
Billy passed away this morning.* I instantly felt a sharp pain
in my heart that I can still feel today when I think about that
moment. Oh no, not Billy, no babe, please not Billy. He's
had a hard life; he deserves to have a better future. I didn't
get to make him his dinner; he really wanted this dinner. He
died alone; I burst into tears, and my husband just held me. I
walked over to the tank and had to tell all his little babies he
was gone. I needed to find them homes from families that
would love them as much as he did. I kept one and named her
Billy; she is still alive and well at 24 years old. My mother
has her and feeds her like a queen; my friend Billy died in
1995, and will forever be missed.

After Billy, I couldn't stand being around this Dr.
anymore. I hated how he treated Billy and the staff. I had
already advanced pretty quickly and became his manager. I
just couldn't tolerate how easy it was for him to discriminate
and insult staff and patients. He knew I was done there, so he
offered to pay for my college education to be a physician's
assistant and continue his practice with him. That was
probably the nicest thing he's ever offered or done. I told him
I would think about it but I knew to make a deal with him
was like making a deal with Satan, and I couldn't owe a debt

to someone like that. Within a few weeks, I found another job and gave my notice. He was very upset and couldn't believe I would leave him. I was happy to leave him and never return. The new medical assistant position was offering more money and benefits. It was at a pediatric office in New Rochelle, NY. I got really good at my job; I was known as the nurse that can take blood out of a rock which was helpful when you had to take blood out of babies and toddlers. I worked there for about two years then got a better paying job as a medical assistant at DOCS in Yonkers, NY. I had to go where the money was because my husband worked, but I always made more than he did, so I needed to be employed at all times.

My husband was talking about going to school to get his CDL license to drive trucks. This would take him away from our home, leaving me with the great responsibility of taking care of our home and kids while he was away getting his education in Syracuse, NY. I decided to support his decision because if he did it, then that would improve our living situation. He decided to do it and off he went to Syracuse, NY to trucking school. He would call me every day a few times a day and come down every weekend to work at a cellular device store and make some money. It wasn't very long before the phone calls started to be less frequent down to one time a day in the evening when he was "going to sleep." Shortly after being there, I can feel the lies increasing. I couldn't prove anything because he was so far away, so I only had a gut feeling and had to take his word for it. I trusted him; I know he used to lie about stupid things, but I don't think he would ever lie to me again or have an affair.

One night, I decided to call him randomly, and he answered but was quickly trying to get me off the phone. I was asking him questions about paying the bills and what the kids needed and how hard it is doing it alone, when I hear a group of girls laughing in the background. I said, *what the hell is that? Do you have females in your apartment?* He said, no, they are here with his roommates and then literally hung up on me. I was pissed and hurt. Could he be doing some shit behind my back? Would he play me dirty even though he knows I don't play that? I didn't hear back from him until the next day. We got into a huge fight, and he told me that his phone died and when he went to charge it; he went to sleep, that's why he didn't call me back. What a freaking lie, but I couldn't prove it. He is my husband, so I am going to let this one slide and move on especially for the kids' sake.

My grandmother loved my husband so much and always had nothing but great things to say about him and defend him. I was still very much in contact with my grandparents even though I was living in NY. They were my everything. My grandmother was a firecracker; she was funny, witty, sarcastic and had a perverse humor which would embarrass you but make you crack up laughing all the time. My grandfather would still give me $5 to buy things every time he saw me. I would say "pop, I don't need it, it's okay." He would say no, buy yourself or the kids something. I had no choice but to take it even though I was married and working. I would go almost every weekend to visit them and my mom and brothers in Stamford, CT.

One day, while I was at work, I get a phone call from my mother at my job, and I knew something was wrong. She couldn't talk, so she made my brother tell me that my grandfather was dead. The man I considered my hero, my dad, and my protector was gone. I started crying in the middle of the front desk and had to be pulled away to a back room so I didn't scare the parents and kids. I called my husband, who was home with us at the time and he came

100

immediately to my job to get me because I couldn't drive or function. It was Wednesday 2/21/1996; a day I will never forget.

I don't remember the funeral; I think it was too painful for me to grasp he was gone. My grandmother told me that he said he wasn't feeling well after he ate and wanted to take a nap and go to the Doctor. after; he never woke up. I saw the disbelief and pain in my grandmother's eyes. I felt for her; they were married over 50 years, had nine kids and have been through a lot in life and now, her other half was gone. She would often tell me after he passed that she doesn't want to be here anymore and wants to be with her old man. My grandmother's life was turned upside down. She now had to leave her apartment and move in with my aunt. She lost her husband and now her independence.

I loved my husband very much and was hoping that he and I can make it through the hard times. It was a challenge, to say the least. He was in school, constantly not answering my calls and hanging up every time I hear a girl's voice. I couldn't believe this was happening and didn't know what to do. One day, when my husband came home for the weekend, I told him that I needed to do our taxes because I was struggling with paying bills and taking care of the kids. He said okay. Then he left for school and that week, when I had a day off, I took the paperwork to H&R block to do my taxes, and they said, *ma'am, someone has already claimed the kids on the taxes, you can't do it.* I was in shock; who in the world stole my information and claimed my kids on their taxes? She looked it up and said, *well, is this your husband's name? In Syracuse, NY?* I said yes, why? She said he claimed the kids and received over $3,000. I'm sorry, but you can't both claim them. I couldn't believe what I was hearing.

101

Could this be true, are you freaking kidding me? I immediately put a call through, and he said yes, I did it. I want to buy a motorcycle, and I knew you would say no, so I did it. I couldn't believe my ears. Wait, you stole the kid's info, went and claimed them on your taxes and took the money we need to survive so you can have a freaking motorcycle? Are you freaking kidding me? He said I don't get to do anything I want or buy anything for myself. I said asshole, you're in school and I'm supporting the family so you can get what you said you wanted. He said, no, I'm doing that for the family. Back and forth we went, I was in shock that my husband basically stole from his own family so he can buy a motorcycle. I told him he better not buy that damn motorcycle when the kids need food, uniforms, and I need help with bills. He said, fine, whatever. Then a few days later, I called him to check in, and while he was talking to me, a friend in the background goes, *hey man, you got the bike, that shit is nice and he turned it on.* I said, *are you freaking kidding me, did you get the motorcycle?* I hear the girls and guys in the background. He said, Yes, I did, that I deserved it and he hung up the phone. I just held my head in disbelief and cried. What a betrayal! What the freak was I going to do now? No money, a shitty husband, working 12 to 14-hour shifts to make ends meet and bills piling up. I had to look strong and be strong, so the boys didn't know what was happening. I was in complete shock and disbelief. The shit was done now, no money but we had a freaking motorcycle in the family.

Here I was, 24 years old and so depressed, lonely and frustrated with this marriage and the joke it had become. I couldn't stand being around him and his selfish ass anymore. He would have the balls to come down at weekends on his motorcycle to show off what he bought via my hard-earned money. I was so ashamed and embarrassed that this is what my husband did to me. I wanted to pay him back for all this shit and the girls I know he was messing around with behind my back.

In my anger and frustration, I decided to go on AOL chat rooms to meet other New Yorkers. It was a dial-up system, so it took some time getting on but it was fun meeting others online and getting away from my crappy life. So, once the boys went to bed, I turned on the computer and started chatting away. On one of these log-ins, some screen name kept popping up and telling me he liked my name. I kept deleting it, but it kept popping up saying *hey there, I like your name*; this went on a few times when I finally said, *okay, thanks*. Before I knew it, we started talking, and I realized how quick and witty he was with his comebacks and answers. I liked it; it's been a while since I had any stimulating conversations especially with the opposite sex. We were logging in to speak with each other almost every night, and before I knew it, we were scanning pictures of ourselves and uploading it to send to one another via email.

I don't know if this guy is even real, but he was super entertaining and fun to talk to. It took me out of the bullshit of what my husband was doing to me. He was still calling me when he wanted to, hanging up when it was convenient and coming on weekends to work when he felt like it. I was stuck in a nightmare. The guy on the AOL chatroom was completely aware that I was married with two boys and super unhappy. I made it very clear to whomever I was talking to on the chat room that I was married and I was not planning on leaving my husband because he's a good father when he's around; shitty husband, but a good father. I figured what could be the harm; it's only through a computer and I was

103

honest upfront about me being married with children, so he was very clear of the situation from the outset, right?

Well, after a few weeks, the chat room and computer pictures weren't enough. We exchanged pager numbers, including phone numbers and started talking in the evening when the kids were asleep. It was so nice speaking to someone without the drama. He had a calm voice; he was really smart and interesting to talk to. Before I knew it, I couldn't wait to get home so that I could tell him how my day went. His name is Rudy, and he lives in NY city. When we would talk, I made sure I mention my husband and kids when I saw an opportunity so we were clear that nothing could happen between us. I think this was my way of not feeling guilty that I was talking to another man behind my husband's back. When my husband would come home on the weekends, I would try and discuss our marriage, but my husband was so damn selfish he treated me like an inconvenience and a nag, which made it easier to talk to Rudy because he treated me with respect and dignity. To make it clear to Rudy that this was going nowhere, I tried to hook Rudy up with my cousin Maria. He was totally not interested, and she was totally against dating anyone from a chat room, so that didn't work as planned.

About four months had passed since Rudy and I started talking. I decided to tell my husband that I was going to see someone else because I can't take him treating me like shit anymore and I knew he was sleeping around on me. He started laughing and said, "Yeah right, you wouldn't dare." I said: "No really, I'm going to start having an affair. I'm not happy with you anymore, and I found someone who makes me happy." He just laughed and said yeah okay, go ahead. I said okay, but I'm not kidding. I'm just letting you know that

I am going to have an affair. He just laughed it off, and we hung up.

Okay then, I told my husband and whether he believed me or not wasn't my problem, so I decided to call and meet Rudy in person. We made a date to go to Red Lobster in Yonkers, NY. I wanted a public place, in case he was some sort of lunatic. He told me he was driving a black Cherokee jeep. I got there early so I can see people driving in and out and if I recognized the car, I was really nervous. I was thinking to myself that I should just go back home, this is stupid and I shouldn't do this. I waited a few minutes then I noticed a jeep parked. I decided to walk up to it, and there he was. Oh, shit, I thought, I think I'm in love with him. Crap!!! Could it be possible to feel like you love someone on the first look? What am I going to do now?

He got out of the car and handed me a bouquet of roses. We went to Red Lobster for dinner; I'd only been there once but I remember it being busy, so it was a perfect place to meet someone with lots of witnesses. We ordered dinner; he had the Chicken Alfredo, and I ordered the ultimate feast. We sat down and immediately started talking as if we always knew each other. Then our meals come out, a small plate of pasta was put in front of him, and my plate came out with two waiters. Oh my God, I was so embarrassed. We looked at each other and started laughing so hard my stomach hurt. We had such a good time in each other's company. We didn't want the date to end. I knew the kids were with a babysitter, so I had time. We decided to see Liar, Liar with Jim Carey which just came to theaters and I heard was super funny. We laughed and laughed; I had the best first "non-date" ever. I drove home and couldn't stop smiling. This felt right and so damn wrong at the same time. I didn't like the feeling of seeing someone behind my husband's back. So, I tried to tell

105

Rudy we couldn't do that again, but while I was trying to stop it, I couldn't stop it. We kept seeing each other; my husband ignored me, and I didn't care anymore at this point. I just needed to figure out how I was going to tell my kids. I spoke to Rudy and told him that if he's serious about moving forward with our relationship, he needed to give me time to tell my husband that I want to go to counseling to separate so the kids could understand what was happening. I asked him to give me a few days to see how I was going to do this. My husband was graduating from the trucking school, so we could discuss it then. I told my husband we needed to talk and he knew exactly what was going to happen and tried to convince me to work it out with him. I told him I didn't love him like that anymore; he begged and pleaded and said that it wasn't fair to the boys. Of course, that was the pot calling the kettle black. When I begged and cried, it wasn't important, but now that he was graduating and was about to lose everything, suddenly it became a priority.

I was adamant that it wasn't going to work after he stole the money from us for his motorcycle, the girls calling his phone, the way he was treating me when he was away at school and the abandonment I felt towards not just me but the kids. He started saying he will sell the bike if that would help. He said the girls weren't anything to him; they got his number from the guys he was roommates with, blah, blah, blah. I didn't care and knew that everything that came out of his mouth was just more lies. He tried that whole weekend; I told him I wanted us to go to counseling. He agreed because he thought it was to help us mend, but I intended to divorce him in a way that he and the kids could deal with it better. I had not spoken to Rudy for a few days because I told him I was going to put us on pause a few days so I could discuss this with my husband. Then I wake up on a Sunday, and my

106

husband is sitting next to the bed on the floor, crying. I asked him what's wrong; he says, "Are you having an affair?" I said, "Why do you ask?" He says, "I already know the answer; I just want you to tell me, are you having an affair?" I said: "Yes, I am." He started crying so hard, but I was not moved. I said, but I told you a couple of months ago that you were hurting me and to stop treating me like crap, and that I was going to have an affair with someone who cared about me and you laughed and wouldn't believe me. I don't know why you are acting so shocked. He got on his knees and begged me to please not leave him. I said I'm sorry; I'm not happy with you anymore. He said don't you want to know how I know you're having an affair? Okay, tell me how do you know?

My husband says; Your so-called lover called me on the phone and told me that he's been screwing my wife and that you are nothing but a whore and I shouldn't be with you anymore. I said 'yeah right', he would never do that. My husband proceeds to ask me then how did he know that my lover was diving today? Your lover, told me he needed to tell me so he called me after he was done diving and you could hear the boat bells in the background. Oh, my goodness! I said, *what's his name*? My husband said he wouldn't tell me, that he told me enough. I don't know what kind of guy you think this guy is but he told me you're nothing but a whore and that he was playing you. I felt like a tiny insect. Like the dirt under the dirt. Did I just give this guy my heart and my trust and he called my husband? Wow, why would he do that to me? I instantly became furious and enraged because of this betrayal. My husband has to be telling the truth because there is no way he would know that Rudy went diving that day. There's no way he would know such specific details. No way!!

107

I called Rudy up to meet him the following day. I was going to the nail salon and asked him to meet me there. I told him, *so you called my husband yesterday?* He just looked at me and said, *what are you talking about?* I said, *well, my husband told me that you called him and tagged me a whore and that I was going to leave him for you. That's great, thank you so much for making this easy for me. I don't ever want to see you again.* He sat there in disbelief and asked me to please not do this. He didn't know what I was talking about. He says he would never call my husband, that he doesn't even know his number. I said yes, but you know my house number, and he knows too many details, like the time you called me and that you were diving, and on the pier, when you called. Rudy tried to explain he doesn't know how he would know that but he would never betray my trust especially when we talked about me leaving my husband to move on with him. I was cold; I cut him off and told him never to call or come looking for me again. It was over, I mean really over! Rudy started crying, asking me to please not do this. I didn't care, what a bastard to betray my trust that way. From that day, I decided to work it out with my husband and try my best to help repair all that was broken. I cut off my pager number and didn't answer any more phone calls. Rudy tried to reach me through my friends, but I told them to tell him it's over and to leave them alone. They did, and eventually, it ended. My husband and I started working on our marriage. For months after, I still had Rudy on my mind every day, but onward and forward, I had to focus on my marriage.

Things started going well between us and the kids. It felt like not too long after that, part of my life started to get on track. It was around this time my grandmother started feeling ill, and we found out she had Non-Hodgkin's lymphoma. She started losing weight rapidly and was very thin, more forgetful and bitter that she was still here without her old man. My aunt was trying the best she could to take care of her mom. It was hard; I can see the exhaustion in her eyes, all while taking care of a toddler at home. Some of us tried to help where we could, but most of it landed on my aunt. My grandmother reverted to behaving like a child. She was demanding, pushy, eating things she was told not to, calling out to my aunt through the night and so much more. I felt bad for my aunt taking all this on, and I felt bad for my grandmother not wanting to be around but having no choice.

For a year, it was on and off with her prognosis, then suddenly, she took a turn for the worse and was put in hospice. She was on a respirator and was no longer talking. We were called to come and see her because she was in her last hours. When I walked into the room, my uncle was telling her not to leave and that she needed to fight to stay alive, which I believe is why she was still hanging on with the respirator. I yelled at him and told him to get out of the room. I bent down to her ear and said, *grandma, you can leave, we are all going to be okay. Go be with grandpa; you don't need to fight anymore.* I saw a tear come out of her eye, and what sounded like a whisper that said, okay. A little while later, she was gone. I felt the worse pain someone could feel when losing a loved one. They were my parents as far as I was concerned. There will forever be this empty place they once occupied in my heart. I do, however, have faith that I will see them again.

My husband stepped up and was very supportive and loving through this process of my life. I was depressed and angry that my grandparents were gone. I wanted my kids to have as much time with them as I had. My grandmother died 1/27/98, and that was also the day of my Ernie's 10th birthday, and the

109

next day was Justin's 4th birthday. That day she passed, we
had a cake and gifts over my aunt's house for both of their
birthdays because we wanted them to not associate any
mourning and depression over their great-grandmother's
passing with their birthdays. We celebrated their birthdays
and her passing from this earth to God. My heart was
rejoicing over my sons' birthdays and crying for the pain of
losing my grandma. We all made a concerted effort that they
will remember that day as a joyful day of celebration.

I was having a very difficult time getting through this. I felt
like I just lost both of my parents and was left alone. I just
existed during the day; then in the evening, I was crying
myself to sleep. I was dealing with a deep depression for
about one month non-stop until one of those nights while I
was crying, I saw a shadow coming towards me, and it was
my grandmother. She touched my face and said, *okay mama,
that's enough; you need to stop crying*. I wasn't even afraid; I
felt comfort. I said, "But grandma, I miss you and grandpa so
much, it hurts!" She said, "We are fine. I promise you, look,
grandpa is waiting for me; we are together." I looked behind
her, and I see grandpa standing in a bright light with his
famous brimmed hat on. I said okay; I'll be fine. I love you
so much! She said I love you too; she walked away. They
disappeared and I fell asleep. I stopped being depressed and
crying that very night. I still tear up when I think about their
hugs and kisses and the love they gave me when I didn't feel
anyone loved me, but I know they are okay and I will see
them again.

I started focusing more on my family and my job. It was time
for me to start thinking about school. My husband was done
with his truck driving school and was home now, working
full time, and things felt normal again. I was a little frustrated

with him still about the motorcycle and his selfishness, but I forgave him and he forgave me, so we decided to move on.

He took on a second job that had him out of the house a lot, and I started ultrasound school, so I would have my brother or my sister stay with us to watch my boys. Ernie was ten years old and very responsible, so I had him pick up Justin from school, and they would be home until I arrived at 5:30 pm. I worked three 12-hour days and went to school in the evening, and my husband decided he would work a lot too. I was pissed because I thought he would at least be home with the kids more often being that I supported his truck driving school away from us.

My husband started fighting with me every day because I was in school and when I was home, I had a ton of homework to do. This was 1998. He started fighting with me more and his second job was as a night security officer in the mall. The kids were always being watched by someone or Ernie, being almost 11 years old, would have to watch his little brother for us. The tension in our home got really bad. My husband was pissed that I decided to go to school. We had pretty vicious verbal fights every day which would give him the excuse to run out of the house in anger. I felt like I was getting hit below the belt constantly in this marriage. Here we go again; I'm feeling all alone and frustrated over his selfishness. I just couldn't understand how he could fight with me about going to school when he did it and left us for a long time. I felt at least I was still working full time and bringing home the bigger paycheck.

1998 was definitely a year of a roller coaster ride for our marriage. In August of that year, for my birthday, he brought me an African gray parrot named Freddie and a huge cage. I stand in front of the cage in shock, I say 'hello Freddie' and the bird replies 'hello asshole'. We all laughed,

111

it was so awesome! Then for our anniversary in October, I took him to Vegas for a week. It seemed like we had just gotten into a honeymoon period after all our fighting. It was now Christmas, and we were celebrating with his family and the kids. Everyone had opened all of their gifts, but he had one more gift for me. He gives me a box with a synthetic rose and I thought the gift was the rose. After thanking him, he told me to open it. And when I opened it, hallelujah, it was a larger diamond ring. I started crying. He got on his knees; I said yes again; what a wonderful loving moment! Wow, we are definitely going to start all over again.

So, I started reading bridal magazines, looking at different venues, and planning things with the kids. I was so excited that we were going to start our marriage all over again and make things new. One day, when we were in the car driving to go to dinner, I pulled out a bridal magazine, and I said look at this dress, isn't this beautiful? To which he replies, "Don't bother me with this stuff. I gave you the ring, that should give me at least three to four months of no aggravation." Holy crap! Did he really just say that? I looked at him in shock, and I said, "Did you give me this ring because you wanted to or did you give me this ring so I can shut the F**k up and leave you alone?"

He said we don't need to speak about it right away. WOW! "Okay then, don't worry about it. I won't bother your ass about it anymore," I replied. This is January 1999, a new year, so I thought.

Then on February 9th, just one month after, as life goes on, I walk into our bedroom, and I see my husband packing a backpack. I asked, "Are you going somewhere?" He said, "Yes, I'm going to go find myself." I said, "What the hell are you talking about? There is a mirror right there; look, you're found!" He says he needs to find himself

112

because he doesn't know what he wants. I said this could not be happening; this must be some sort of joke and I am getting punked right now. He says no, that he is leaving, that he does not know when he will be back.

I could not believe what I heard. I thought we left all of this shit behind two years ago. How in the world do you get up and leave a wife and two kids to find yourself? So, I sat there in disbelief. What in the world is happening right now? I felt like the whole ground went out from under me. I waited a few hours after he left. I called his brother to look for him and his brother didn't know where he was. I called his mother to look for him and she didn't know where he was. I told them what happened and they couldn't believe it. I called him several times and he would not answer the call. I didn't tell the kids; I made them take their baths and put them to bed, and then I went to my room and just cried. Late in the evening, I called him and he picked up. I said, *what in the world is happening right now, do you have another woman*? He said, *no, I'm just not happy and I need to find myself. I need to find what makes me happy*. I said, *you are married with kids, you need to figure it out here with us*. He said he is not coming back home. So, that night, I cried myself to sleep, alone!

I got into a severe depression. I couldn't function normally. I would come home and literally throw myself on the kitchen floor because walking to the bedroom was too much work. The kids were struggling pretty bad. Their father and I started fighting viciously over the phone quite often. I was tired of begging my husband to come back home and him not wanting to. My kids were struggling. Ernest was 11 years old and Justin was 5. Ernest started to eat a lot to hide his feelings and was quickly gaining a lot of weight. Justin started wetting the bed at night and was having behavior

113

problems at school. I didn't know what to do; I was left with two boys, an apartment, a car note, student loan, and bills. He completely disconnected and wasn't helping me.

One day, out of the kindness of his heart, he took the car that was under my name and gave me his older car that didn't have a car note, so he could pay the note on the newer car and help that way. I still couldn't believe this was my life. I was so depressed I could hardly function. I would get the kids up for school like a zombie. I had to give my 11-year-old the responsibility to take his little brother to the bus stop and pick him up after because I had to work and go to school and their father was always busy "working" and didn't want to help.

It wasn't hard to find out he left us for another woman. My sister-in-law told me about this chick he was seeing, and I knew it, but I couldn't catch him. It was so hard to understand what was happening; I was so tired and lost.

One day, I went to work and when I got home, my husband had already come to the house and took things; he basically robbed me. He took my sports cards collection that I had started collecting for Justin when he was born; he took my brand-new expensive DVD player and DVDs to bring to his new apartment with his new woman. He even went into my dresser and stole the ring he had just given me in Christmas. Who does that? You leave me; then you rob me? I called him right away, and we started fighting so badly. My little Justin started jumping up and down in front of me and yelling, "Mommy stop, mommy, stop it, no more, mommy stop." I said okay baby, and I hung up the phone.

Then I got down on my knees and I hugged my baby boy, and I told him I'm very sorry and that mommy and daddy love him very much, that we're just fighting. Justin says, "Mommy, call daddy and tell him he can come home;

114

I'll be a good boy. I will listen and I will not fight with my brother." Oh, my God; my heart broke into pieces. I looked at him and said, "Sweetheart; none of this is your fault. Your father left because he wanted to, not because of you. You are a good boy; mom and dad just fight too much."

Of course, I had to find out who he left us for and I found out that he was dating her for over a year. She was only 17. So, the reason he left us in February was that she had turned 18 that previous November. So obviously, he was waiting for her to turn 18 to leave his family. Now it was clear why I never saw the money from the security job. She was the "second job" he was telling me he had this whole time. That was such a hit to the chest!

Here I am, a 27-year-old woman with two kids, competing with a 17-year-old girl. Mind you; my husband was 30 at the time. The level of insecurity I got was horrible. She was younger, thinner and had no kids or baggage.

How in the world am I going to tell my kids about this girl? I was so ashamed and embarrassed. He didn't waste much time bringing her around his family and friends. Showing off his new prized possession. I was livid, to say the least. I wanted to hurt him so bad.

My boys were confused as to why this was happening. I wanted to tell them that their father was an asshole who only cared about himself and I hope he died somewhere but that wouldn't be nice. So, I just told the boys that he loves them, but he just doesn't love me anymore. That stung my heart like crazy. I felt lonely and now self-conscious about my weight, looks, and career. It felt like everything I thought and knew about myself wasn't real.

I was so pissed at my brother-in-law because I thought he and I were close, yet he knew the whole time about this bitch, and he never told me. So, I realized that we

115

are not that close of friends. Therefore, I exposed his affair to my sister-in-law as well. F-it, if I was in pain, I wanted everyone in pain with me. Not the right thing to do, I know, but I wasn't worried about it. I just wanted revenge.

Now I had to try and find a new way of coping. I felt so empty that my 7-year relationship and marriage was done without warning or preparation. I was feeling afraid to be home alone, especially at night so I called my cousins Maria, Liz, and Bren to come over, keep me company in my home and sleep over on the weekends so I wouldn't be alone with my thoughts. My husband was taking the kids to his mother's house every other weekend and I was going crazy thinking about them together. How did I not see this little girl come in to destroy my family?

My thoughts were getting the best of me, so, I called a friend of mine name Jay, we became friends after Billy's passing. I knew he was a religious man into a sect called Santeria. Santeria is a religion that worships African saints as powerful beings that take your prayers and request to God. When he explained it to me, it seemed innocent, so I started getting into this religion. It didn't feel foreign to me because in the Catholic Church, there are lots of statues and you light candles to them, so why was this any different. It's custom to have two candles, one to the statue saint and one to Jesus. The rituals can be from a few days long to a few weeks long, depending on how bad you need their intervention. I fully got engaged with this religion when my husband left because I felt void. I felt like there had to be something more than what I was experiencing. My friend Jay started guiding me on praying rituals, blessings, spells and things like that. He was always trying to convince me to do curses, but I knew that was something I didn't want to get into. He tried to have me invite some high priests into my home to do a "cleaning"

116

with chicken's blood, but I always knew in my gut not to go too far. I was always going to Botanicas, which are special stores where you pick up the articles you need to pray and do your rituals. I also had to get my tarot card readings, tea leaf readings, palm readings as part of the religious traditions. They even wanted to make me a priestess in the religion because I was very intuitive and could at times tell them things before they told me and I could feel a different spiritual presence around me, good and bad. They were trying to hurry and make it happen, but I refused to go that far. Something wouldn't let me.

Doing all these rituals and prayers helped me not think about the shit show my life had become. I started to come out a little bit of the depression and anxiety. My husband was now living with this girl, everyone knew it and I had to accept it.

Chapter 4

TIME TO MOVE ON….

After almost two months, I decided to go back to AOL chat rooms and take my mind off all of it. I decided to stop crying and entertain myself. So, I developed a habit that every time I got the kids to bed, I would turn on my computer and log in. I had terrible insomnia anyway, so I might as well kill time. Then one day, I logged in and I get this message, "Oh my goodness, is that you?" I didn't recognize the screen name, but my heart leaped! Could it be him? I screamed like a little girl, *okay Neena, take hold of yourself, maybe it's him, but maybe it's not*. Um…I answered, *maybe it depends on who this is*? And I waited, covering my eyes but leaving a crack between my fingers so I can see but not see. Then he says, hi, it's me, Rudy! I jumped off the chair and ran around my room like I was in the Olympics, screaming silently so the kids wouldn't wake up. *Okay, Neena, keep it together, act cool*. "Hey there, long time no see, how are you?" He asked, "Fine, do you still have the same number?" I didn't, so I gave him my new number, and he called. We spoke for hours and hours. Suddenly, I heard a baby crying in the background, so I asked, wow, is that your baby? He says, no, I'm babysitting for a friend.

Now that my husband left me for another woman, I was free to talk to him as much as I wanted. Damn, I missed him so much! About a week or so of talking on the phone, he met me at Dunkin donuts right after one of my ultrasound classes. I had gained more weight, so I didn't really want him to see me, and he looked the same. That same feeling of love I got the first time I saw him was the same feeling I got this second time we met again. This time, there was no husband on my part; I wasn't sure if he had a wife or kids throughout the period we were apart.

He looked at me and said, "I've missed you every day we were apart, you broke my heart, and it nearly destroyed me." I felt so stupid, "I was so sorry I did that. I really thought you called my husband and told him I was a whore for sleeping with you and you were going to take the kids and me from him." It wasn't until recently that I caught him listening to my messages and when I called the pager company, they told me that my pager was programmed to forward my messages to his pager first, then it will notify my pager a few minutes later. He was able to do that because he worked for the pager and cell phone company. I felt like such a dummy when I found out. I asked him, and he admitted that he did listen to all my message first for months and that's how he knew Rudy was diving that day, but he had to do it not to lose his family. Of course, now that he left his family, he didn't care if I knew.

This was now April; my husband had done a shitload of things to us since he left in February. He robbed us, abandoned us financially. I could barely get him to be involved with the kids, let alone watch them while I worked, but why stop there?

One day, while I'm at work, I get a phone call from the bank telling me that I had to return my car for lack of payment. I was in shock. My husband gave me the old car and took the newer car so he could make the payments to help the kids and me, right? Right?! Asshole!!!

I asked the bank rep. "Wait, are you saying that there have been no payments made to the car at all in the past few months?" She said, "That is correct, and we need to pick up the car; it is going to be repossessed." I agreed to have them come and pick up the car the next day. I called my husband and was screaming and yelling, did you literally not pay the car note? Now, I'm going to have it repossessed because of you! The car is under my name; this is going to ruin my credit! Oh well, he says, sorry but I didn't want it anymore. Well, they need to pick it up tomorrow, and I just got the new rims for that car, you need to bring it here tomorrow so they can take it. He said, *okay, I will*, and the next day, I see the car in the driveway and the tow truck pulling it away. I couldn't believe this crap. This guy has no end to how many times he's going to screw the boys and me over. Who is this guy? I felt like such an idiot to have believed anything ever that came out of his mouth.

While all these things are happening, at the same time, things between Rudy and me started going really well. I introduced him to the kids after a few months. Of course, my husband found out I was seeing someone, so he comes to my house to start a fight about it. I look at him in disbelief. "Didn't you leave us? What the hell gives you the right to come to my apartment and tell me I can't see anyone when you are living with your girlfriend?" He looks at me and spits in my face. I was so hurt and humiliated. He knew what my ex did to me, and he just did the same thing because he knew it would hurt me. I sat in shock for a few minutes then told him to get the hell out of my apartment.

He was furious; he picked up the boys that weekend, and while he was with them, he convinced them that what I was doing was wrong and that I should go back with him. Now, it was around August and my birthday was coming, Rudy and I were having a great time together. The boys liked Rudy, but they loved their father more. They came to me and said, *mommy, you need to give daddy another chance. He's changed and he wants to be back with you.* I told them, no,

121

but they insisted that if I loved them, I would try because they want their family back together.

I was so mad; I knew that the kids were being manipulated, but they were upset and wanted me to try. So, I broke it off with Rudy to work it out with my husband. I just wasn't in love with my husband anymore. He lied to the kids and me and was still living with his girlfriend. This time, I was the second job. I knew he was still with her even though he denied it. I just couldn't look at him the same anymore; he was garbage, and I knew it. One day, I was home and my husband came to the house, and after a few minutes, he looks at me and says, *you want to be with Rudy, don't you*? I said *yes, I don't love you anymore.* He said *okay, I am not going to force you to be with me if you don't want to.* What a relief.

So, I explained to the kids that we don't love each other like that anymore. And now, I had to try and get Rudy back!! I missed him, and I hurt him again for the second time. I was able to contact Rudy and explain everything to him and that it will never happen again. Rudy forgave me, thank God, and we started dating again. The kids were having a great time with Rudy. He took us on his boat, and out to dinner a lot. The kids were starting to get spoiled and my husband didn't like it at all.

He comes to pick up the kids for his weekend, and he tells me that he's the father and he will do whatever he can to make sure the kids always remember that. Rudy will never have a chance and he's going to make sure of it. I said, *so you will make the kids miserable because you want to be a selfish asshole*? He didn't answer, and he kept his word. The kids started changing towards Rudy and making statements I knew didn't come from them. My ex was succeeding in driving a wedge between my kids and Rudy. I was trying to mend it on one side, but it felt like a losing battle. Rudy and I

122

were very happy, and we spent lots of time together, along with the boys. I was finishing school and doing some internships for ultrasound. When 2000 rolled around, we were living together in my apartment in Yonkers, and he was running back and forth to Jersey every day to run his own business car detailing and car accessories called VIP automotive boutique.

I had to finalize the divorce with my husband, so I found a place that helped me do it myself without a lawyer having to get involved. I did it, and I got divorced. Finally, the paperwork went through! Rudy and I planned our wedding; we paid for all the bridesmaids' dresses, $6,000 in flowers, and my dress that was $5,000 on sale. We had a lot of fun planning such an amazing dream wedding. Rudy told me his clients gave us tickets to Australia for our honeymoon. Wow! My last marriage was a nightmare, so I was so excited and looking forward to this day!!!

Rudy and I got married on June 16, 2001. It was a wedding I will never forget. Let me tell you about this amazing, wonderful, adventurous day that will forever be engraved in my heart and mind. The day of my wedding, I was in the hotel upstairs, getting my hair done and I noticed that our announcement that was on the TV was no longer coming up but instead, another wedding was coming up. That's strange; they must have confused the banquet rooms. Just then, Rudy called me and asked me to come downstairs to the event manager's office. I asked why, that I am getting my hair done and so are all the girls. He said it's important; I need you down here right now. So, I got dressed and went downstairs. We had 200 people coming to the wedding, so I'm not sure what could be so important just a few hours before the wedding. Our original wedding planner was amazing, and just before this day, her husband had a terrible

123

stroke, so she quit her job and this was a new guy we never worked with. We just had an amazing rehearsal dinner here the night before where we spent over $1000 on food and entertainment for our wedding party.

I get to the office, and one of the women who knew us from the previous meetings was standing there at the door with a face stricken by fear. I said hello and walked in, and Rudy was sitting at the table with the new guy. I said hello, *what is so important that it can't wait until the wedding*? He says, *sorry, we are canceling the wedding*!!! WTF did you just say? He says the check we have was a business check and they can't accept it. They need cash or a cashier's check. I just looked at Rudy, and he had his head down. I looked at him and said, *what the hell is this guy saying*? Where in the world do you expect us to go and get a cashier's check for $43,000 on a Saturday afternoon when we have people staying here and people that are coming from all over? He said, *well, sorry, that's what we need.* Are you f***ing kidding me? We were here last night and spent a ton of money why didn't you say anything yesterday? He says *well, I just got the info.* I instantly started crying. He says he understands. I got up off my chair and went to his face and told him you don't f***ing understand shit. I wanted to hit him and Rudy so bad. I ran out of the office, and the woman that was standing at the door cleared the way for me; she knew better than to say a word to me. He says he can let us have the wedding in the smaller banquet and when our guests give us wedding money, they will take it instead of the check. My temper hit the roof, *get the f**k out of my face before I commit a crime.* At the same time as I was crying outside on the steps, the florist came up and was like, *hey, I just heard what happened. I'm so sorry.* I just paid this guy $6,000 in flowers and I didn't see a damn pedal even though

124

he knew what just happened and we called him for weeks after with never a return or call or response. It turns out they were best friends.

I was beside myself. I had to call 200 people to tell them the wedding was off. I couldn't believe it. I was angry, numb, frustrated and other emotions I can't explain. Even now as I write this, I need to stop to take a breath and clear away my tears.

In the midst of my crying, the pastor we hired to married us said, *weddings are about you two, not all the stuff. I have a friend that owns a restaurant on the water just a couple of miles from here, and I called him, and he has agreed to host your wedding for you. It's not this fancy, but this is about you two.* I said, "What about all the people that are in the lobby waiting for us?" He replied, "I will take care of it." I couldn't face anyone. I was so embarrassed and, in more pain, than I ever felt before. I got myself ready and the wedding party came with me. We were going down the glass elevator, and I see all my guests waiting for us. I started crying; I got off the elevator and started walking towards them to scream what a piece of shit move the hotel just did to me, and Rudy grabbed me and said *no, we are going to get married and you are not going to do this right now.* I wanted to scream at the top of my lungs and hide at the same time.

We went to this seafood restaurant that was packed with guests; they lead us to the back of the restaurant which was the deck and the wedding party went out there—a few friends including my ex-husband and his girlfriend and my beautiful boys. There was a couple there celebrating their 50th wedding anniversary. Ernie walked me out to give me away to Rudy. I could barely feel; I was so broken. I feel like I just went through the motions. I was in so much pain, and even today, it stings. How could such an amazing day

125

become this? Don't I deserve it? Don't I deserve a dream wedding like everyone else? I guess I'll never be able to get this day back. And we never tried to do it again. When this happened, I called one of my girlfriends that was part of the wedding party and told her not to come because of what just happened. She says I deserved it trying to have a big wedding and show off like that. That now, who is going to reimburse her for the money she spent to get her hair and nails done? WOW, that stung so badly!!! Why wasn't the reaction, oh man, how are you? I'm on my way? I love you and know that I support you? I mean she didn't even ask me what happened and how I got screwed over by some con artist. Friends, who need them anyway?

I had taken a month off work to spend with my new husband and the boys. I couldn't tell you how depressed I was. It was so bad I forgot about the trip his clients gave us to go to Australia. I was literally crying every day for what seemed like the whole month. Rudy was trying to take me out dancing, to socialize and clubbing as much as we could. We made plans like 3-4 days a week to go to Stamford to hang out. I started playing games with the boys, going to the movies and spending as much time with them as I could. In the evening, Ernie would watch Justin for me, and I asked my neighbors to just keep an eye on them from time to time. The boys filled me with so much joy. We did weird things like eyelash fights, dancing in the middle of store aisle for no reason, sing and play beats and we thought it was completely normal to break out in a song in the middle of a conversation. I remember the week before I had to return to the two-faced people at work. Ernie, Justin and I laid down together and watched *Mulan and the Emperor's New Groove*.

It was a constant struggle to get out of my deep depression, but as time passed, it seemed to be getting better.

My cousin Bren was getting married herself, so I went to the bridal shower on July 15th, 2001, this was only a month after my disaster wedding but I needed to support her, so I went. We had Rottweiler puppies at this point; Rudy and the kids watched the puppies while I was at the shower. Then he took the boys to miniature golfing and Applebee's restaurant. Rudy was trying to be closer to them, and I was grateful for that. Then when we all got home that night, I decided I was going to try and be fancy and make flaming bananas with vanilla ice cream. It was delicious, but I didn't get it to flame up at all. I was trying not to think about the fact that I had to go to work tomorrow after a month of being away and getting phone calls from "friends" at work telling me all the horrible lies and things people were saying about me at work. People actually made me feel bad, that they were mad at me, about my wedding. Pretty twisted, huh?

Well, I needed to pray to the saints. Rudy was completely against my religious choice of praying to saints but didn't want to disrespect me, so he just went along with it. At this point, I was into Santeria for about 2-3 years. Here I was, having to face these fake ass people and I needed all the help I could get. After praying, I realized that I couldn't change what happened the day of my wedding and I am no longer going to apologize for inconveniencing people on that day. I give up. I hate what happened to us and the way we were treated, but now, I know who my friends really are. No one asked me if we were okay or if we needed anything. Lesson learned! I have to get out of this depression and stop letting this take over my life. It's just too painful to keep thinking about. So, I started the boys in swimming classes, and I couldn't believe how fast they were catching on. I needed to focus on my family and not the everyday crap that people I worked with were doing and saying about me, but

127

what other choice did I have? I have to help pay the bills and take care of the family. My depression was becoming my friend and my enemy. I was frustrated a lot and quickly. I was feeling neglected by Rudy who was working a lot. I think most of it was to avoid watching me go through my mood swings and lash out. Can't say I blame the man, but I did.

Ernie had me occupied by telling me to read the *Harry Potter* series with him so we can talk about it. So, I did. Finished the first book and started on the second. I loved it. Nice to get away to a fantasy world.

Summer, Summer, Summer, time is here. I need to get out of this funk. So, in August, we took the kids, my niece Gill and my cousins' daughter, Dez to Great Adventures, Hurricane Harbor in New Jersey. Then we came home and dropped off my cousin's daughter in Stamford. We were going to Karaoke, but it was boring, so we came home. Here come my lows again; I just don't know what to do with this unhappiness. I hate my job; I can't remember what I've learned in ultrasound school and I feel like such an idiot. My memory fails me often, and I am getting more and more moody and angry about it. I started to doubt Rudy as well. I feel like I'm being let on and something is going to happen, and I'll find out something terrible. I pray I'm wrong; we just got married but everything done in the dark comes to light. Right?

Well, it's my birthday on August 10th and Rudy surprised me with a nice dinner at "La Lanterna" in Westchester NY, then a party at "Latin Quarters" in NY city, and lots of our friends, my brothers Frankie, Edgar, Edgar's girlfriend, and my aunt all went to surprise me. It was so nice; the place gave away our table by mistake, but instead of letting that piss me off, I just went dancing. I felt like, the story of my life, first they take my wedding and give it to someone else and now my birthday table. It's another hit against me, but whatever!! I feel like life is just making me it's punching bag.

Well, now, my friend Dee was getting married in a few months, and I was part of the wedding party; believe it or not. So, it was her Bachelorette's party, and they had a stripper named Bobkat. Dee and her friends couldn't get enough of him. I went way to the back because this is not my thing. Plus, lots of these women were the ones that talked about me and made me feel like crap because of my wedding disaster. Even my "friend" that asked me who was going to reimburse her was part of this wedding party. I was trying to be cordial as best I could but damn, it was hard to be around someone who was so damn selfish. My friend got married in the first week of September 2001. It was a nice wedding, and I tried to get over my disaster of a wedding memory and celebrate hers.

I needed to get out of there. I told Rudy how hard this was for me. He made reservations for that week and we took the boys to Medieval times in Lyndhurst, NY. It was so much fun and the boys really enjoyed themselves. It felt so good to see my boys and my husband getting along, enjoying each other's company. Ernie and I were always talking about *Harry Potter*'s books and the movies that were coming out; I am on my third book at this point.

So, on the second week of September, I was at home on my day off, and Rudy calls me around 9 am and says *honey, please turn on the TV, I'm driving over the George Washington Bridge to NJ, and there is smoke coming from NY city. Can you turn on the TV and tell me what's going on?* Oh My God! As I watched the TV, I saw that one of the twin towers was hit by an airplane and is on fire, and suddenly, the

129

second building is also on fire. The first plane crashed into the first building around 9 am; the second airplane crashed into the second building around 9:18 am. The news is going crazy; they are suspecting terrorists. As the world is watching the news, another plane crash in Washington D.C at the Pentagon, our center military base. Our country is under attack and I'm watching it on T.V. live; the news says that the White House is reporting messages of attacks. I started panicking. My kids go to school here in Yonkers along the Hudson River. I need to get them. Are we in a war? Now, Rudy is in New Jersey and the bridge, the airports, the train stations, the buses, all of it is closing because they don't know if there will be another plane being used as a bomb. I can't believe this is happening; I don't know what to do. I can't get in contact with Rudy anymore; the phones aren't working well. Dear Lord, please help us. Don't let these evil people prevail and invade us like this.

Then as I looked on, the second building starts to crumble and come down. I started crying, and you see the shadows of what looks like bodies jumping out of windows. Dear Lord, please hear our prayers. The first trade center building is still standing but engulfed in flames. They just confirmed that 158 passengers and ten employees were on the plane that hit the first building. Now, they are saying that the al-Qaeda organization is claiming responsibility for this horrible attack. So many people gone, so many families destroyed. Oh my God, as I watched Fox news, the first building crumbles and fell over; the twin towers are gone... Gone!!! Now, they are saying there is a fourth plane that has been hijacked and may be headed towards the White House, and a possible bomb just went off at the NYU medical center. I was terrified; this is the most devastating thing I have ever seen in my entire life. Now they say there was no bomb at the medical center. I got dressed and drove as quickly as possible to my kid's schools; my boys were in different schools, and by the looks of it, every parent in the area had the same thoughts I did. There were cars everywhere picking up their babies. I'm so scared, but I tried to tell the boys it will be okay.

As stupid as it sounds, we went to the grocery store to get some things for dinner because I just didn't know what to do with myself. I didn't want to panic; the boys and I were so worried because I haven't heard from Rudy. Lord, help us, we are at war! Now, they are saying that it's the work of a man named Osama bin Laden. I pray President George Bush Jr. and the military gets him and he dies a horrible death. The whole country stood still.

To top this day off, my landlord comes upstairs a few hours later and says he wants us to move out by January 1st; he wants the apartment for the family. Are you freaking kidding me right now? I just looked at him in disbelief; I had no words. I can't believe this is the day he chooses to tell me this shit. I don't even know where my husband is and if he's okay. I needed to pray to my African saints and God to help us through this.

I let the boys play video games in their room because my depression set in like a black cloud and I didn't want to infect them. I was so tired and fatigued and couldn't concentrate or formulate complete sentences. I was lying in bed wide awake the whole night, waiting, then finally, I heard from Rudy extremely late that night. Thank God he was okay. I had to tell him the fantastic news; he wasn't happy that we need to move in 6-8 weeks right after Christmas and in the middle of winter. This marriage was getting hit below the belt since the beginning.

131

As the days went on, I was trying to be as normal as possible by cooking for the family and going to the gym to meet with a trainer. We decided to watch a movie called "Joe's Apartment" with Ernest and Justin. It's a funny but gross movie about roaches. I'm so grateful for my family and the fact that we are okay. I feel so heartbroken for the ones who've lost their loved ones. I pray they get the resolution they deserve. Rudy, Ernest, Justin and I went to the front of our home and lit a candle for a vigil. My street had many homes that lit candles for the victims, volunteers, and workers helping the country with this tragedy. It's only been nine days since this tragedy, and I'm having violent nightmares of war and fear of terrorists. I send my kids to school with a knot in my stomach every day.

As time went on, we started to go through such stressful situations. Rudy was having trouble with his business and the owners of the building; we were with no money and had to move. WTF are we going to do?

I don't think we can withstand one more freaking thing to happen. Since we got married, it's been one shit-show after another. How much can one family take? Our faith was being rocked. It's now just October; Christmas is around the corner. We have to figure this all out. We are so short on money and everything feels like it's going to shit.

I was even afraid to open my mail because the terrorists are now sending random letters to people with anthrax and people are dying. This attack is causing lots of us to experience some PTSD.

Time keeps ticking and I don't know what we are going to do. Now, it's the beginning of December, and our Landlord wants us out by next month!! My ex-husband took back the car that I was using to get the kids and me around. I couldn't do anything because this car was under his name;

the car that was under my name he got repossessed. Unbelievable, I really hate this asshole! We had no health insurance, no money; our cell phones got terminated for lack of payment, no money for rent; Rudy's car was getting repossessed and so much more. We are in a desperate state.

I need to pray more…so one day, I was doing one of my ritual prayers. In this ritual, I was praying to an African saint that has a stone with a face carved into it and a black candle alongside a red candle with the picture of Jesus on it. As I was holding the lit match in my hands to light the candles, I looked at the Jesus candle and felt like I was awakened by something. Almost like looking at those coded puzzles that make you look hard to find a figure and suddenly, it becomes clear, and you see it. So, I looked at the Jesus candle and said, "Wait, Jesus am I doing something wrong?" I felt such a conviction that I couldn't light the candles. I blew out the match and felt lost. I fell to the floor of my bedroom and started wailing, G*od, what is happening? Am I doing something wrong? Lord, please show me if what I am doing is the wrong thing*? I fell asleep crying on the floor and never did my prayer to the saint that night.

The next day, Rudy dropped me off at work because I didn't have my own car and almost at the end of my shift, I get a phone call from my little guy who says *mommy, this is an emergency*. I said, *what is it*? He said, *the house is on fire*. I screamed, "Get out of the house." He said *we did mommy, we have the dogs, we put the birdcage out on the porch, but we can't find the cat*. I ran out to the parking lot to jump into my car when I remembered I don't have a car anymore. I ran back into the office and asked everyone if someone would take me home immediately. I got a ride home, shaking the whole way, wanting to jump out of the car and run as fast as I could to get my babies.

133

The fire department had already stopped the fire. It was December 10, 2001. Six months after my marriage, 15 days to Christmas, my husband just lost his business and was closing it that very day. We are now homeless; we had no money, no business, no place to stay, one car, depression and anxiety that was nearly debilitating. I felt like the man Job in the Bible.

I thought…is this God or spirits coming after me to destroy me because I didn't pray and turned my back? I looked at the hole that used to be my kids' bedroom and said, *God, if this is you, this ain't funny.*

It was freezing at around 21 degrees; we slept in the back of the house which was our bedroom with a plug-in heater and in our car to keep warm. The next day, I took out our renter's insurance papers and called the company, and they said, *we are so sorry ma'am, but your policy expired months ago.* I couldn't believe what I was hearing; I made her double check, and she said we've been canceled months ago. I hung up and started wailing to the point that I couldn't breathe. I was desperate. So, I took the paper in my hands and said with my voice trembling and fear running through my body, "Lord, if you are real and you prove it to me, I swear I will follow you all the days of my life."

We slept in the car that night because it was really cold. We came upstairs in the morning and I felt numb. We are trying to gather and pack the remainder of the apartment and trying to figure out what in the world we are going to do and suddenly, we hear a knock at the door. I didn't want to open it because it must be the landlord to make sure we are getting ready to leave soon.

We open it and it's a stranger, so I asked him if I could help him. He introduces himself and it happens to be a man from our insurance company. He asked if we were the

134

Perez's and I said yes. He proceeds to tell me that he reviewed our renter's insurance policy and there were some misunderstanding…we are fully covered! I couldn't believe what I heard; was this beauty in the middle of the mess? I looked at my husband in disbelief and relief and said, "He's real, God is real!" I was fully convicted in my heart, and I knew right there that I had to keep my word that if He proved to me that He was real, I would follow Him. But where do I begin?

The insurance agent assessed all the damage as we were standing there with the smoke coming out of our mouths from the hot breath hitting the frigid air. He looked at us and seemed moved by our situation and gave us a check for some emergency funds so we can find a warm place to sleep and shower. I wanted to hug him, what a relief. I sent the kids to be with their dad so they wouldn't have to be going through so much. After one night, their dad gave them back because it was his birthday and he wanted to go to Boston. Damn, you would think that he would maybe take them with him or not go at all to protect them from all this hurt, but no, just the kind of man I wanted to marry.

So, off we went; my family took the first part of the check and went to a hotel in Nyack, NY. We were cold, hungry and homeless. We just wanted to go to a hotel with our cat and find a place to eat. We locked the cat in the hotel bathroom and out we went with the kids to get something to eat. When we got back, I saw the cat was out of the bathroom, so I told my husband we must have left the door opened and thought we closed it. We thought it was weird but didn't give it a second thought.

We went back and forth to the house to care for the animals and stayed in the hotel one more night, then we gathered our things and left to drop off the kids to their dads' home and go back to the freezing apartment to check on our turtle and African gray bird and the dogs which we had to leave there because we couldn't take them with us. We brought Billy the turtle a heater for the tank and covered it with a thick blanket. Our bird was covered with another blanket, the best we could to keep him warm, and one dog we kept with a space heater and the other dog in his doghouse on the deck which was insulated well. We had a Christmas tree in the dining room which was still decorated with an American red, white and blue theme—my poor attempt to be patriotic because of the attacks on the twin towers.

Our boys' gifts for Christmas were spared mostly in the fire, so we asked my cousin, Maria, if we could celebrate Christmas at her home. We had at least 6-7 gifts per kid. I always started shopping for gifts in September, so when December came along, they would have a lot to open.

When we got home, we were stopped by the landlord and told that he doesn't want the dogs at the house anymore. So, he called the dog patrol on us for having the dogs outside. He was hoping they would take the dogs. I agreed and told them I would keep them inside, but then, the landlord's wife came and told me we couldn't keep the dogs in the house anymore. I told them that they had to understand that we couldn't keep them outside because of the dog patrol and it was freezing. She said it's not her problem. In which I said, actually it is. You guys hired some guys off the street to do the roofing job and use a freaking blowtorch, and they started this fire which could've taken the life of my kids. They just looked at me with a blank stare. I walked away because I was already down and out. I didn't need this crap, and I didn't want to go to jail for violence. We told them we needed more time; we were waiting for the rest of the insurance money to move. They said no, and we said we are staying until I find a place to move. The landlords refused to give us back the deposit because he had to fix the house. What the freak? Back and forth we went, trying to make our case and they make theirs. I just didn't have the energy to keep fighting, so I told them to shove it. What goes around comes around. We might not have been the best tenants in the world, but we deserved compassion for something they had a fault in and almost killed my children.

So, we had to wait on the insurance money and hope it comes soon so we could get the heck out of there. I felt like this has to be someone else's life; I was numb! We just lost our home, had no car, my husband lost his business, my kids weren't staying with us, nowhere to go, fighting with my landlords, no money and little hope!! Holy crap! There's no way this could be happening. I felt like dying, just ending it all. I broke down and started crying; my heart couldn't take it anymore. My depression worsened, and my anxiety spiked all the time. I would wake up in the middle of the night with sweats and felt like someone was choking me.

We stayed in the home, cleaning it out, packing and trying to figure out what we were going to do as the days counted down to our eviction. A couple of days later, as I was going through the things we had in the hotel stay, I noticed that our jewelry bag felt really light, so I opened the bag, and we realized we had been robbed at the hotel. Whoever came into our room while we were at dinner stole all our expensive jewelry. My diamond rings, my diamond tennis bracelet, my husband's diamond cross pendant, his expensive watches and left the jewelry bag with the costume jewelry, they literally stole approximately $30,000-$40,000 worth of jewelry. It was all we had of any worth besides my family and animals. I look at my husband and say, *that's why the cat was out of the bathroom when we got back*. I knew something was

137

wrong. We had spoken about selling some pieces to survive. I couldn't believe what was happening. I know it had to be the hotel attendant because the room wasn't broken into, someone had a key card. We called the hotel right away and told them what happened. Of course, they denied everything and filed a report. Yeah right!!!

I called my cousin Maria and asked her if we can stay with her. My mother didn't offer to help in any way, so I didn't ask her. Thank God Maria said yes and we went to her home for a couple of days in Stamford.

We didn't want to be intrusive, so we left all of their gifts at Maria's home. All of us on Christmas Eve—my cousin, her daughter, Rudy, the boys and me went to my aunt's home. My family stayed with my aunt and the next day, my sons' father picked them up to spend Christmas day with them, and we agreed to open all their gifts when they got back. So, a day later, we had our Christmas at my cousin's house and stayed over that night so we can be together as a family, then we took the boys back in the morning to their father's home while Rudy and I tried to find a place to live with the insurance money.

Thankfully, my other aunt that lived in Bridgeport was going away with her husband for the New Year's week from 12/29/2001 until 1/4/2002, so she asked if we could house sit. We jumped on that opportunity because we didn't want to be a burden to my cousin who was so gracious to take us into her small apartment. We got the boys and stayed with them so we could feel somewhat normal in a home like a family. While we were staying there, we got a phone call from a realtor from William Pitt. We got his name from my aunt. He wanted us to go and look at a few houses that have come up for rent in Stamford. We immediately went to look at the homes because we wanted to be able to do it with the boys while we have them. We're desperate to find something before we had to find our next place to sleep. As we were searching for our home, we all fell in love with a beautiful little home on Knapp Street in Stamford; it's called the Springdale area, very nice and clean, not like Yonkers at all. It had three bedrooms, a very small kitchen with a lime green countertop, living room, dining room and a tiny room off the kitchen that we would make into the kids' playroom. So, we put in a bid for the house to rent and on January 2nd, the realtor told us that the landlord accepted our offer, but we didn't tell the boys we got it until we went to sign the lease. Then on Saturday, January 5, 2002, we had our first night there together as a family, the timing was perfect.

After a few days, I applied for a new job in Stamford and got it, and after a couple of weeks of commuting, I quit my job in the Bronx. I had terrible anxiety attacks sporadically through the day, and it was too hard getting back and forth to work from Stamford to the Bronx every day. Rudy was out of work but had some side gigs in Jersey. My baby brother, Edgar, had already gotten married and had a beautiful baby girl named Steph just a few weeks later. She was so darn cute. I was so happy that he started a family and I love his wife. She is so good to him and for him. It was nice to see that we were all moving forward in life.

Thankfully, we had enough of the insurance money to pay for rent, bills and to buy some beds, a couch, and some household items; things started feeling normal again. Then after a couple of months of living in Stamford, I told my aunt what I felt with what happened with the burning of our home, being robbed, and about the miracle of the insurance agent coming through even when they said we weren't covered. I explained to her that I promised Jesus I would follow Him if He showed me He was real and He did show me, so now I need to keep my word. So, she says *well, I went to visit a nice church in Darien CT, but it's not Catholic.* I said *okay, I'll go. Please take me this Sunday.* So, when Sunday came, we met her in Darien and went to this charismatic, non-denominational church. It was in an old dinner theater, so it definitely didn't look like any Catholic church I was used to. We found our seats and we were standing for praise and worship, but it felt so foreign to us because we didn't know the songs, and it was long. How many songs do they have to sing anyway?

Once the worship was over, we sat down, and the pastor started the preaching; it was actually really good! During his sermon, he stops and says, "God is telling me that someone here has been worshiping saints, getting tarot card readings and messing around with the occult. You need to come down here for prayer." I couldn't believe what I was hearing; I looked at my husband and said, *did you tell someone about my Santeria?* He said, *how am I going to tell anyone anything? I do not know anyone here.* I was stunned; I stood up and started walking down to the pulpit, and to my surprise, so did 70% of the church.

The pastor came off the stage to the altar and started praying for people and putting his hands on their foreheads, and some were passing out. I was like "oh, hell no." I don't know what that's about, but I am not falling out for no one. Then he got close and put his hands on my forehead and said something about breaking the curses over my life or something like that. I can't remember exactly because I felt an electric sensation throughout my body and I fell to my knees even though I was trying to be strong. I tried looking around the room, but the tears in my eyes were so thick I couldn't see where I was and I felt like I was drunk. What the heck just happened? I tried to get on my feet but was

140

wobbling and disoriented for just a moment while I tried to find my husband on the seats where I left him. I came back to him, and he says, *are you okay*? I just started crying because the power I felt come through my body was nothing I have ever felt before, and it was overwhelming. I was judging everyone who was passing out at the altar, and this humbled me greatly.

After that experience, I wanted to know more about this God. I was about turning thirty that year, and I needed to do something different with my life. My life was so hard and unfair. I wanted to know, so I asked God, "Where were you?

God, where were you when these things happen? Do you exist? Did you love me?" My grandmother always made sure that I would go to a Catholic Church, especially when I was with her, which was more often than not. She made sure that my mother baptized me when I was an infant, that I did my first communion and my confirmation. My grandmother made sure that I attended Catholic Biblical studies when I was a kid and that I regularly confess my sins to the priest, which I totally hated. I'll never forget the one memory when I was done with confirmation, and it was time for me to go into a private room and confess my sins to the priest. I looked at my grandmother and said, *why do I have to confess to a man who is probably a bigger sinner than I am*? She slapped a spit out of my mouth. So, I went into the room and confessed! I was always seeking though in my youth. I remember my mom letting me go to a few events with friends of hers. I went to Kingdom Hall with Jehovah witness; I went to evangelical Youth and children's classes. I guess wherever she can send me to get me out of her hair when I was a child.

God, I want to heal and all of these areas of my life thus far. I invite you to come and show me where you are in these memories and exchange the pain that I feel for the love that you have for me. I know that these things happened to me, not because of me. I know that you are all-knowing, all-encompassing, all-loving, and a just God. I give these hard childhood memories to you, and I receive your just and perfect love in each of these memories.

It's amazing how vulnerable you are as a child and how easily terrified you are and how quickly the evil actions of others can implant a root inside of you that you carry most if not all of your life! *I also have a lot of trouble sleeping still. I'm always afraid that somebody's going to be standing over my bed when I open my eyes or behind the curtain when I'm in the bathroom or shower. I hate living in fear; I need you to take away these fears. I am no longer a child; I am an adult.*

This is now 2002, a new year, new jobs; new schools are coming for the boys and a new life in Stamford, CT. We started going to church regularly, joined a Bible study and on the weekends, we still go out to clubs and have our drinks here and there. The Bible study leader, Lucy, told me, *come as you are, if you go clubbing, keep clubbing, if you smoke, keep smoking, if you drink, keep drinking.* I thought to myself, *cool, I don't have to change a thing.* She said you should only change because God told you to and you want to, not because someone told you to do it. Best teaching I ever got; it comes with no judgment and puts the responsibility on me.

Chapter 5

WHAT NEXT?

As 2002 was moving along, we had our ups and downs. I was working at the medical office in Stamford; Rudy was doing little construction jobs and some car work on the side, still not finding a full-time job but trying. He is always complaining about headaches and not feeling well. I think it could be some depression from all we've been through in this past year.

The boys started attending Stamford's public schools. They were so happy because they didn't experience the bullying here like they did in Yonkers. We spent much more time together, and Rudy's son, Christian, also spent more time with us and even moved in for a few months. He was around ten years old and so adorable. He even called me mom which I loved! It was nice having three boys. Rudy and I talked about having maybe one more and hopefully a girl.

It started going well in Stamford, and we loved this house on Knapp Street. Our Rottweilers were doing well, Bishop and my female, Chanel; she was pregnant again with another litter on the way, very exciting.

Suddenly, Rudy was invited to go to different military events because he's a veteran, so he was always dressing up in his military suits and leaving in the evenings, but I was happy for him because this was something he loved. I would stay home quite a bit with the three boys and watch movies, make dinner, let them play video games and then I would go to bed reading a book to help me go to sleep. I used to love the Flowers in the Attic series or anything Stephen King wrote.

For the boys, everything was starting off great; they loved their schools. On the other hand, Rudy was still not working consistently, so money was getting really tight again because we spent most of the insurance money trying to get our household together. I was having anxiety and depression and working on getting through it.

Fall was here, and it reminded me that we were getting really close to Thanksgiving and Christmas, and I was super excited about that because I could decorate this home the way I wanted for the holidays and actually have family over.

Last year was a tough year. This year is going okay so far. It only has to get better…Right?

So, I thought…Well, Rudy was going out a lot to these supposed military thingies,' and I was left at home to look out for the home and the boys. I'm not too sure what's going on with Rudy, but he's out of character. He's also not feeling well a lot and grumpy and cranky all the time with headaches, always snapping at the boys and me. I was about done with him and his attitude.

Thanksgiving was here! I was so excited; we had Thanksgiving and we invited our family over. It was a ton of fun to entertain like a real family. It was snowing outside, and Rudy and I thought it would be a great idea to buy a deep fryer to fry our first turkey. We had to put it outside because it was a propane tank fryer. Rudy had to pick up my family, so he asked if I can watch the fryer with the turkey in it and if the temperature goes down to make sure I check the turkey because it can overcook. I said okay, I'll watch it. He left, but it was so snowy and icy on the deck. All I did was peek in through the sliding doors. I thought to myself, the turkey was big, so I'm sure it's fine. I kept cooking the side dishes. About 45 minutes later, Rudy comes home and says "hey

144

babe, where's the turkey?" I said, "Oh, it's outside." He yells, "What!!! Are you kidding me? That Turkey should've been done a long time ago." I said well, it's snowing and icy outside, I thought it would be fine. So, Rudy goes out and gets the turkey out of the fryer; he just stands there for a second looking at it. Sadly, the turkey that started out about 12 lbs. now looked like it lost some weight, maybe around 6 lbs. Rudy looks at me and says, "Babe, we can't serve this!" My aunt says why not? It just looks a little overcooked; it's not that bad, even though you can see the bone coming out the wing. When she goes to pull the wing to try it, it literally became a poof of ashes! Then she took the piece and started crunching on it, and it disintegrated. Yikes! I just started laughing so hard I almost peed in my pants, and everyone joined in. The freaking Turkey was ashes to ashes and dust to dust! Needless to say, we never again fried a turkey, and Rudy still brings it up every year; I will never live it down!

Christmas was next and I was super excited; it's my favorite time of the year. I told Rudy that I wasn't sure what I was going to get my new little niece, Stephanie. Then Rudy goes under the bed and takes out all these little outfits for a girl. I said why in the world do you have all these girl outfits? He said he knew I would want to get my niece something, so he got these in the city on sale and wanted to surprise me. I said that is really sweet of him, and thanked him. Then I prayed, *God, this doesn't feel right, please let me know if there is something I need to know.*

A few days later, Rudy comes to me in the bedroom and says, *honey, I need to talk to you about something serious.* I said okay. He proceeds to tell me that he has a daughter. A little girl born in 1998, right before we got together. I felt like my world just crumbled before me. I stayed stunned for a minute, then I said, *that's what the clothes were for, wasn't it? For your little daughter. Why didn't you tell me about her? What the freak is wrong with you*, and I jumped up and smacked him and started crying. I felt so betrayed. I kicked him out of our bedroom and just sat on the floor crying. I had so many mixed emotions. I was glad it wasn't while we were together that she was born but upset that he never told me. I also remembered when we spoke on the phone so many years ago, I heard a baby crying in the background, the one he said he was babysitting. When I asked him if that was her I heard crying so many years ago, he said, yes but was terrified to tell me. That makes her about four years old. Damn it, another hit to the chest.

I didn't speak to him for a few days. He knew better, so he left me alone. I spent most of those days praying about what to do, and while I was praying, I felt like I heard God say, this is the little girl you've always wanted and that calmed my anger right down for some reason. I went to Rudy and said, *I'm ready to meet her now.* He said, *are you sure, you don't have to.* I said, *bring her here, I want to meet her and her mother.* So, a week or so later, this amazing, little, tiny Asian-looking girl comes into my home and completely stole my heart. Her name, Stephanie, just like my niece, the name I loved. This little princess gives me the biggest hug, and I immediately bonded with her in my heart; she became mine. Within a month she was living with us, and I couldn't be any happier. I couldn't even be mad at Rudy anymore because I felt like God gave me this gift.

Then one day, getting ready for the Christmas season, I was downstairs in the garage taking care of the puppies and Rudy comes running into the garage with his face all scraped up. I got so scared; I asked: *babe, what happened?* I thought someone attacked him outside the house. He says, *I don't know babe, I was cleaning my car and I saw black and*

146

passed out, I woke up in the driveway. Jesus, what is going on? I was so scared for Rudy. I made him come inside so I could clean up his face.

I had Rudy go to see our Doctor the next day, and he sent Rudy to a neurologist to see what was going on and to possibly get an MRI. We had an appointment for the MRI the day after Christmas. I was so nervous that something would happen to Rudy driving, but we were trying to be cool about it for the kids. We spent Christmas in our new home together with all the amazing decorations and all the kids' home to enjoy as a family since last year; we didn't have a home.

A few days later, Rudy's neurologist calls us into the office for the results. Rudy is very nervous, and so was I. We went into the doctor's office, and the doctor told us to be seated. As we sat down, the doctor said, *I got the results from the MRI and I'm sorry to tell you that you have a condition called vasculitis of the brain.* He proceeds to pull out the MRI to show us what he was talking about. He points to a certain area of the brain and says this vessel is completely closed, and this vessel is double the size, trying to make up for the vessel that is closed. That is why there is a lack of oxygen going to your brain and the reason you're having blackouts, passing out spontaneously, and massive headaches. Rudy and I just looked at each other in silence for what felt like an eternity. Rudy was shocked. I looked at the doctor and said, *okay, what do we need to do*? The doctor looks at us and says, *unfortunately, there really isn't much you can do.* The doctor proceeds to say there is an experimental surgery that they can do but it absolutely won't do anything, and it will just be for exploration. Rudy has got about 40 to 50% chance of dying on the operating table. Rudy leans forward and says, *there's nothing we can do?* The doctor replies, *unfortunately, it's too far gone, so I am going*

147

to put you on a cocktail of medications to help you not have so much pain, not black out so much. I am sorry to say that I predict you have 1 to 2 years left.

My husband just sat there in complete shock and pain. I looked at the doctor and I said, *I rebuke what you are saying in the name of Jesus my Lord and Savior. I know that God can heal all things, and I believe that He will heal Rudy from this.* The doctor looks at me and smirks a little bit and says, *oh, you are one of those.* I said *yes, I sure am. I thank you for your expertise but my husband will not die, and he will be healed.* Rudy, on the other hand, was not with me completely when I said this. I think he thought I was a little crazy as well. I just refuse to believe that what this doctor was saying is the truth; my brain could not compute. The doctor gave us the MRIs and the prescriptions that he would have to take a couple of times a day to help him cope with the prognosis he just heard.

We went home after picking up his medications at the pharmacy, and we looked at each other, not knowing what was next. What are we going to tell our kids? I just refuse to believe that this was what God had planned for us. There's no way; there is just no way this can be happening. I was certainly not ready to let him go.

As the weeks went on, Rudy became almost unbearable to deal with. He was angry, hurtful, combative, and completely checked out of the family. We told a doctor of what was happening, and he said it was the medication, but that was a cocktail that worked to help him. I was trying to be as patient as possible because I knew this was a very scary time for him and all of us.

Around this time, he got some very bad news that his older brother was dying of a rare leukemia that he got from contamination for helping in NYC at 9/11. His brother needed both Rudy and his sister to be tested to see if they would be a match and be able to give him t-cells. It turned out that they were both a match but Rudy's sister is really petite, and the Doctors said that this would be too dangerous for her to take these shots and give t-cells. Rudy was his only hope. Rudy's family expected him to do it because he was the only match, but Rudy was scared because he himself was just given a death sentence and he didn't think he could take this, and it would kill him faster. Rudy also made the decision not to tell his family about his diagnosis because he felt it would be too much for his mother and father to bare. His sister was furious with Rudy because he didn't respond right away. I didn't want Rudy to do it because I didn't want anything to happen to him and his brother was cruel to Rudy and abused him as a child.

But my husband, being who he is, decided he would help his brother fight this even if it were the last thing he did. So, he had to take these Neupogen shots twice a day to increase his cell count so he would have enough to spare for his brother. This meant stopping all his medications while he did this and being in severe pain in his entire body with nothing he could take to relieve it. This was almost unbearable; I wanted him to stop because seeing him in pain every day was ripping me apart inside.

Through this, Rudy had gotten more disconnected, was going out and staying out all hours of the night. We barely had a marriage left to hold onto. I knew in my heart that he would be healed, but he cannot accept that. He thought I was living in la-la land. Of course, the pressure of trying to save his brother while his family watched and not knowing Rudy's condition and us trying to keep the family together was mounding and my sons were fighting all the time and it was getting really bad. So, his son Christian

149

decided not to come back when he was at his mother's for the weekend. That hurt Rudy very much because if he is dying in a year or so, he wanted to spend as much time with his son as he could.

Thankfully, Rudy was able to create more cells than his brother needed after one week of treatment, but unfortunately, even after treatment, we lost his brother because the cancer was very aggressive.

This caused my husband to be angrier and more unbearable. We continued to go to church because I think that was the only point of sanity in our lives at this point. And one of the evenings, when we were at church, we had a guest pastor coming to preach. He was preaching about the power of God, and the healing power of God, and then he stops the service and says, *God is telling me that there's somebody here who is having a very serious problem with his brain. If that is you, I need you to get down here so I can pray for your healing.* Rudy pushed me out of the way. I have never seen him do that before; I think all of these months of pain, anger, frustration, and being afraid was mounding up to something he could no longer sustain. The pastor put his hand on Rudy and prayed over him. Once Rudy told them what the problem was, I was crying; Rudy was crying, and I just knew that he was healed. Rudy did not completely accept that he might be healed, so he continued to take his medication, but this time, the medication was giving him adverse effects. He started to cut down the medication because it wasn't really doing what it was doing before. It wasn't helping him with headaches like it was supposed to. We were about nine months in this battle, and I think Rudy got to the point where he was now or never, being that the doctors were saying that he had maybe a year or two to live. Rudy's headache started to dwindle significantly; his moods

150

got back to normal. I definitely saw a change and so did he. He stopped all medications, and we just believe that God did what God said He would do.

Chapter 6

WHAT NOW?

So, a year passed and then two years, and my husband was still here, praise God; he was definitely healed! Rudy had another MRI done to check the vessels and see how it was, and it was gone, GONE! The Doctor turns to me and says, *'well I guess you serve a good God'*, to which I replied, *"Yes I do"!*

That was a hard hit to our family but we got through it. Now, Rudy had trouble finding steady work because the construction business is so difficult, so we had to move out of that home we love so much into a smaller apartment, and the most hurtful thing in the world was that we had to get rid of our dogs because the landlord who was one of our leaders at the church didn't accept dogs in his apartments. I was completely shattered, not knowing what to do without my Chanel and Bishop? I took them to this wonderful organization called Paws in Norwalk and literally within a day or two, they were adopted to other families separately. That shattered my soul, even now as I write about it, the pain feels fresh.

I started working at a medical office in Norwalk not far from home; the boys started school in Norwalk, and Rudy started working in a company that didn't pay him what he was worth, but it was a steady income. Our little princess, Stephanie, was still living with us, so she had her room and my two boys—Earnest and Justin shared a room, and we had our own room as well. Although this apartment was much smaller than the former house, we made it our own. We're still struggling financially, always having to say no to the kids when they want something, always robbing Peter to pay Paul so that our electricity wouldn't get shut off. It was so difficult to constantly be with your nose just above water, financially. Lots of fights, lots of love, lots of different experiences and a lot of spiritual growth as well for all of us.

Time sure does fly, and now, it's already 2005. I am still working at the Doctor's office in Norwalk; it's going well. Lots of drama working around all those women but I like the Dr. I work for. Rudy started his business up again called VIP automotive boutique. He had this business in Jersey before it closed and now was launching it here in CT. There were a few leaders at the church that wanted to help out and be partners in it. Rudy didn't think it was a good idea; I thought it would be a great idea because they were leaders and he needed the help. Sadly, we were struggling financially, so Rudy had to keep taking contracting jobs so we can eat, and the partners were meeting on the days he had to work and making decisions as if he was just an employee and not a partner. So, as hard as it was, within a few months, the partners took the business from Rudy, and he was left with no business, no say and no partners. They kept everything, the truck, the concept, the business plan, the whole thing. Since they were the ones that got the investment and Rudy wasn't involved in that, they had the rights to it all. Rudy was crushed and quickly went into a deep depression with anger and anxiety attached, something he created and dreamed about for so long was gone, and we had to see the truck around town with his logo on it. Talk about salt in the wound.

Summer quickly came, and Justin has decided to go to his dads for the summer and is thinking about moving with him and his wife. I hope he doesn't go; I really love that boy, and his father is a piece of crap. Ernest started working at

153

Cold Stone Creamery and is thinking about college and what he wants to do.

But the one I'm seriously pissed off with is Rudy. Rudy just told me that he is letting Stephanie move back home with her mother because her mother is furious that we claimed Stephanie on our taxes and didn't let her mother claim her again like we let her in the past. Are you freaking kidding me? She lives with us, why in the world would I let that woman claim her on her taxes; she doesn't even pay child support? Rudy couldn't give me a straight answer. He looked terrified but wouldn't confess to me what was going on.

Here we go again with hiding things from me. The last time he did this was when I found out about the existence of Stephanie; I asked him then if there was anything else he needed to tell me, but he said no.

Now, I see something is up and he won't tell me. I was crushed; my little princess was being ripped away from me and I didn't know why. I wanted to kick Rudy's ass for acting like such a punk and not fighting back. I didn't understand why he wasn't doing anything about it. I am not her legal mother, so I was completely helpless.

Stephanie didn't want to go; she cried and cried but no one gave a shit about how she was feeling and how I was feeling, so off she went back to live with a woman that gave her up within weeks of meeting me, all for f'n money. She left our home on 7/2/2005, a day I will never forget. I cried for months.

I had my kids on and off throughout the summer. Within a few weeks of summer, Justin told me he has decided to live with his dad, and that's killing me. Steph is back with her mom and we get her every other weekend; I miss her so much. I just want to punch her mother in the face every time I see her. I'm trying to get through the pain and

154

move on. I just enveloped myself with the choir, church, Bible study groups and anything else that will keep me from hurting my husband or this woman.

Then on August 3, 2005, my husband calls me to tell me some very terrible and horrifying news. Our pastor's son, who was seven years old, drowned in a pool in Playland, in NY on a ride he was on. It rocked our world! The entire church community was hoping for a miracle and a resurrection. I felt so horrible for our pastors. I couldn't imagine what this felt like. Gosh, I can still feel the sting of that day. I started to pray for the protection of my children and I was thinking, if this could happen to these amazing pastors, this could happen to any of us. It certainly humbled many of us that we are all vulnerable to this life and unexpected tragedies. The whole church was feeling this way. We just wanted to surround them with love, gifts, compassion and anything we could to help them however we could.

I felt for them so badly, all I could do is pray for them and be there as much as they needed me to be. Sadly, this tragedy was too much for them, and the stress of it all ended their marriage eventually, and our first lady left the church, and the women of the church were left without their pastor.

While all of this was happening outside our home, in our home, I also felt for our family. I felt like a ticking time bomb. Since Justin left to live with his dad, he was becoming so disrespectful and resentful. He was recently diagnosed with ADHD which he was not happy about because the medication they gave him made him feel like a zombie and he didn't like it. Christian didn't want to ever come over our home again; Stephanie was being brainwashed not to desire to live with us ever again. The only one hanging in there was

155

Ernest. I was proud of him, he worked, went to church, choir, and paid for his own driving school.

Well, as time does, it keeps ticking whether we want it to or not. It's now already November, and my kids are still not home with us. I was hoping this was all going to be temporary. Stephanie was going through lots of emotional changes and was telling her mom she wanted to live with us, but her mom would not allow it; she even started to keep Stephanie on weekends we were supposed to get her, and of course, Rudy wasn't doing anything about it. So, I prayed, God, if Rudy is hiding something that is making him act this way, I need you to expose it because I am so angry with him, and I don't feel like I want to continue in this marriage. Well, a few weeks after this prayer, Rudy came to me to tell me more truth about his life. It turns out that she and Rudy were legally married and she's been threatening him to tell me because they possibly weren't divorced yet. WAIT!? WHAT? Then our marriage isn't legal. I just felt nothing! Absolutely nothing! I was so numb to all the lies and the deception, and because of it, I lost my daughter. So sick of it all. I had no words; I asked God to expose it, and I got what I asked for.

We went through so much between 2005 and 2006, being evicted because our landlord sold the home and the new landlord wanted all the tenants out. We couldn't afford to move, but here we were again, having to move or be in the street. We started praying to God to provide all the finances we needed to move. Because God is so faithful, we weren't forced to pay rent because of the mishandling of the new landlord and that gave us the finances we needed. We finally moved into a really cute house in Norwalk on Creeping Hemlock, one of the neighbors from the same apartment

156

building where everyone was evicted moved into the finished basement which helped us pay the high rent.

As we were going through this, my son, Justin's grandfather had been fighting cancer and passed away. I was helping my son deal with the enormous amount of pain that caused him. The day of the funeral, my son, tried to jump into the ground with his grandfather because he didn't want to live without him. They were inseparable, and this was beyond his understanding at 12 years old, and trying to explain to a child that loss is very hard, but God is good, is a very difficult thing to balance so that they don't misunderstand and develop hatred towards God and blame Him for everything that's gone wrong. This was new territory for me, and I wasn't sure how to handle it. I gave my son a journal and made him write his feelings in it. I also told him that he needs to try to understand and rejoice that his granddad accepted Jesus as his Savior before he died and that we will see him again. I'm sure he thought I was crazy because rejoicing was the last thing he felt. He was pissed off at the world, and I let him express that every chance he wanted to. I still haven't mastered how to do this properly with a devastating loss.

A few months after this in 2006, I had a dream with my son, Ernest, and in this dream, it was revealed to me that Ernest was hiding something. So, I waited for Ernest to come home from work and I asked to speak with him. I said Ernest, *I had a very unusual dream that we were hiding in dark places. I feel like you are hiding something from me, what is it*? Ernest looks at me and says, *Mom, I'm gay.* I said *what? Are you sure? I think you are just confused.* He said, *no mom, I am gay. I've known that I am gay all my life.* I said, *well, you will not be bringing any boyfriends in this house; we will*

157

not accept that type of behavior and sin in this house. He said, *I know, mom.*

I felt devastated. How can my son be gay? Didn't he know that was a sin? I didn't know what to do. I was so angry inside; I didn't express it then, but it started to come out in my actions towards him and my comments about how he needed to be careful, so he doesn't get AIDS. I told Rudy what happened and Rudy said, *okay, so what*? We need to love him. I was so upset that Rudy wasn't on my side that this cannot be tolerated.

A few days later, we were called to the church by the pastor, and he sat both my son and me down, and said, "Ernest, I was told that you had on your social media that you are gay, is that true?" Ernest said, "Yes, I am." My pastor said, "Well, first off, God loves you, but He doesn't love the sin. So, I am going to have to ask you to sit down from choir until you go and get some help." Ernest said, "Okay, so I can't sing in the choir anymore?" I said that is correct, Ernest, because we need to help you with this. Ernest just looked at me. Then the pastor suggested a ministry that was in the city that helped people with this condition. Ernest reluctantly accepted to go with me to these meetings for transformed homosexuals. That Sunday, the pastor did an entire service on sexual sin and Ernest got up in the middle of the service and left; he never returned to the church again.

No matter what I did to convince him, he was just really hurt that he couldn't worship anymore, that everyone in the church was judging him and that the pastor did a whole service about it and embarrassed him. I took Ernest to the meeting in the city, hoping they could get to him, that he would leave there completely transformed and renewed and he would be back on the choir within a month. This was just a phase.

158

Ernest and I started fighting every day. We couldn't stand being next to each other. He hated me for judging him, and I hated his choice of not wanting to change. He even dares to introduce me to a boyfriend; I wanted to get up from the couch and smack the shit out of him. I told him to get that boy out of my house. The fighting got really bad. Then one day, while Ernest was at work, he told me he had a rash and couldn't understand why. I told him, *have you gotten checked for AIDS? AIDS causes rashes.* He said, *mom, just because I'm gay doesn't mean I have f**king AIDS. You're so f**king stupid.* I was furious, who in the hell did he think he was talking to? I drove to his job to beat the shit out of him, but he had already left. God saved him.

Then that night, I was in a choir rehearsal and afterward, I went to my car and started crying in front of the church. I said, *Lord; I can't take this anymore. I'm done! I'm cutting off my son. Since he wants to be disobedient and disrespectful, I do not want him in my life anymore; I'm cutting him off*!!! And as soon as I said that, I heard an audible voice from God in the car say, *DON'T YOU DARE CUT OFF MY SON! You are the only connection he has with me, if you cut him off, he will not have a connection.* I immediately started crying and repenting. Oh my God. He is God's son first before he was ever my son. God loves him so much that he put me in my place. God said, *you dare judge My son, the only difference between his sin and yours is that his is exposed!* I felt like a little ant under the dirt. I realized at that moment that my close-minded religious mindset was about to destroy my relationship with my son and my son's relationship with God. I had to call my son and tell him I was sorry and he needed to understand that this was hard for me but I had no right to judge him. I was regretful for my behavior and my religious spirit. My son understood and

159

forgave me. I had to tell him to respect the fact that I can't see him with a man; I wasn't ready. He understood and I am so grateful to God for stepping in and helping my ignorance in this matter. It turned out that the rash he was getting was a reaction to the new detergent he was using to wash his clothes. I felt so stupid for the way I behaved and judged my son. I wept, and it took me a long time to forgive myself for my bias and small thinking. His brother, Justin, already knew the truth and loved him the same way he did before he knew and here I was, a full-grown adult, not knowing how to be a good example of love and acceptance.

Around this same time, we were also dealing with my daughter's biological mom taking us to court to get sole custody and for us not to have visitation rights. She was furious that Rudy told me the truth and we were still together. She wanted so badly to destroy our relationship, and she nearly succeeded many times. Then in 2007, while I was praying, God told me it was time to call her and apologize for any hurt I have caused her in her life. I was like, what? That can't be God because if anything, she owes me an apology. Then a few days later, my daughter called Rudy and asked him if he called her mom because my name, N. Perez, came up on the caller ID? He said no, but he will ask me. So, when he told me, I knew it was a sign from God, saying I needed to call her. Yuck! I didn't want to do it, but I knew better than not to listen to God, so I called her. I told her I was sorry for any pain I had caused, and she proceeds to tell me that she never meant to hurt me; she was upset that Rudy never gave her the things he was giving me. I talked to her about how unforgiveness will destroy her and every relationship she will ever have; she needs to release her anger towards Rudy before she causes herself or her daughter any more emotional harm. I realized God was releasing me from unforgiveness also. I hadn't been intimate with Rudy for over a year now because I was still so angry. I invited her to church, and she agreed to come; the conversation ended well, and I suddenly felt compassion for her. She kept her word and did come to a church event we were having, and she gave her life to Christ. Now, I really had to be kind to her because she became God's daughter.

Chapter 7

LEAP OF FAITH

Justin is back living with us for now; he was constantly going back and forth from his dads to our house. When he was mad at his dad, he came home. When he was mad at Rudy or me, he went back. I was frustrated because I wanted him to learn to deal with his issues instead of running away but his father didn't support that, so he would let Justin go back and forth as he pleased and it just infuriated me to no end.

Stephanie was coming to stay with us on weekends and summer vacations but not a day longer than was allotted by the courts. Ernest is trying out for Berkley School of Music in Boston; we still don't see Christian anymore because every time Rudy calls to speak with him, his mother gets on the phone and says, *well, if you love your son, you would've been with us and not that woman.* Rudy loves his son, so he just kept being their punching bag and come Christmas and birthdays, when they needed anything, he drops what he's doing and goes to see him in the city when they allow it.

As for me, I was trying to keep my sanity and forge ahead. I have been feeling like I'm supposed to be doing something different than medical; I was enjoying selling Pampered Chef products, then I went and registered my business as an LLC on April 24, 2007, The Kiddie Kitchen, 'Where Every Kid Can Cook'. I had no idea how to run a business but God gave me this vision in a dream, so I wrote it down and registered the business.

I felt the shift in the atmosphere; I've felt like I'm supposed to go back to school to be a chef, but that doesn't

162

make sense. I was planning on going to go back to get my registered nurse degree. This other stuff was for extra income. I now started having terrible anxiety attacks at work. I was sad, angry and confused about what was happening.

One day, I had a breakdown after work and was crying because I felt so unhappy with the work I was doing. I was praying desperately. I said to *God, okay God, I can't tell if this is you talking or me. So, if this is you, I tell you what. If you come down here personally and tell me that I am released to quit my job and go back to school, I will do it. But you need to tell me personally that I am released.*

About 30-45 minutes later, my husband comes home from work and tell me that he was in the car praying and that he felt like he heard God tell him to "go into the room and tell your wife that I said, she is released!!" Say what?! I made him repeat it because I couldn't believe what I just heard.

I was so shocked, and instantly, I started crying in awe and excitement! That was a tangible God moment. A moment where God felt closer and more real than ever! So, I went into the next room and typed up my letter of resignation; my last day would be September 1, 2007.

Now, I have never done anything this crazy before; I had no plan B. I said, "Okay God, now I have no money, no job, and no idea, what I'm going to do? But I did hear that Fathers pay for their kids' tuition. You are my only father, so I need you to pay for my tuition." When I was in prayer, I felt like he wanted me to go to NCC, so I did, and when I applied for school, I also applied for a scholarship, and I got both. So, there I was, a student at Norwalk Community College, starting on September 4, 2007. The funny thing is, my oldest son, Ernest, was starting college with me, because he didn't get into Berkley, even though his audition went really well.

163

Suddenly, I was in my first class, one of the oldest students in the program with all these teenagers. I never thought I would go to college, especially at the age of 35. My husband was supportive because he knew what God said to him and he wanted to be as obedient as he could, but this left the burden of the household and all of us in his hands. Construction wasn't doing too bad in 2007; he had lots of contracts to look forward to.

2008 was going to start off really great, my husband and I were back on track, and our love seemed to have been growing even more daily. Our kids were living with us except for Stephanie and Chris; they liked school, and we were all getting along for the most part.
On New Year's Day, 2008; we went to a service at our church, and a guest pastor was praying over me, and he said that this year would be the year of my father. That God will show me that he is my father and that God is purifying and cleansing our home. So, I prayed, *okay God, show me that you are my father and cleanse my home.* I looked at Rudy and said, *I hate praying those kinds of prayers sometimes because things happen that come and rock my world. I just hope God also gives me the endurance to take on whatever happens.*

Then I kid you not, on January 2nd, the very next day, all hell broke loose in my house, and I discovered that Rudy has been lying to me for years about a lot of things. He confesses to me that he had an affair. That he is not the man I think he is and tells me he can't lie anymore. He tells me that all those nights he said he was going to the military engagements, he was in porn shops or at bars hooking up with people and having an affair. That the people he told me about and said they were his friends, I never met them because they do not exist. That he just needed to go to the

164

bars and porn shops, so he made them up and used the stories as excuses to get out of the house.

Holy shit! He proceeds to tell me that when we were getting married, his clients didn't give him a trip to Australia for us; he made that up and on and on he went, exposing everything he had done and how many people he hurt by lying, but that he can't do it anymore, that God won't let him live a life of lies. I literally got up off the chair and punched him nonstop like ten times. I wanted to inflict as much pain as I could; he was crying and I was crying, and my whole life crumbled. I pushed him out of the way and went into the other room and started doing my homework, completely disoriented and in such wrath. I no longer had feelings.

He came out of the room and went to his nephew and my son and told them how sorry he was about everything he has ever done to them and everybody. They leave to go to church and seek guidance from the pastors because they can't believe what's just happened. Rudy leaves the house and texts them to ask them to please always take care of me. Then it's radio silence. Well, they got so scared they called the police because Rudy was going to commit suicide and no one knew where he was. I was so indifferent I didn't care at all either way. Rudy finally comes home a few hours later; the kids were so frightened that he would hurt himself. The cops were waiting for him and took him to the hospital to be admitted for suicide watch. I really didn't give a shit. I was all done with this.

I went into my room and said, *okay God, I'm so done and I know that you will not be mad if I leave this piece of crap of a man.* I thought you said this was the year of my father? I guess it's because you don't want me with a liar. Now what? Suddenly, I hear very clearly in my spirit, *go to Jeremiah 29:11*, and I say what is that, what are you trying to

165

tell me? So, I took my Bible and it says: *For I know the plans I have for you," declares the Lord, "plans to prosper you and not to harm you, plans to give you hope and a future.*

Are you kidding me? What does that mean? I prayed to you yesterday and look at what's happening? A future for who? Plans to prosper me and not harm me, to give me hope and a future? I'm leaving Rudy ASAP. And I clearly hear God say, *no, I am making him new for you.*

Agggggh, I just screamed at the top of my lungs. Are you freaking kidding me? I hate him. He's a liar; I hate liars. I was in so much pain; I loved him and hated him all at the same time. I felt like I was grieving and lost a loved one because I didn't know him at all. It was like sleeping with the enemy.

A few days later, Rudy was released and told he must go to see a psychiatrist which he started doing right away. I started going to marriage counseling with him as recommended by our pastors and Rudy's Dr. I started to learn a lot about Rudy and the intense abuse he went through as a child. So many years of much mental, physical and emotional abuse at the hands of his father, older brother, and cousins. My anger towards him started to become compassion because I started to see him the way God sees him, as a hurt child in a man's body, trying to be loved and accepted at all costs. I didn't realize how deep this pain and hurt ran within him. It was so hard for me to trust him because every time I was with him, I saw images of him with other women. I had to constantly pray for God to give me the strength to get through this and show me why God wants me to stay with this guy. God wasn't kidding when He said it was the year of my father and deep cleansing. He started the process right from January 1. There were so many nights when I wasn't talking to Rudy, and I would hear him wailing

166

in the garage, asking God to take away the intense pain he was feeling. It was astonishing to hear; it sounded like someone being stripped of their own flesh. I never heard any cry like that before. This went on for months.

Everything was such a process; I was finding a way to heal; he was trying to find his real self; the kids were learning to trust him again. His family was talking badly about him, and he could hear them; our friends and church family were all talking badly about him; it got really hurtful and bad for Rudy. Our pastor didn't allow him back to the church until he said it was okay. We had a few friends that stayed by his side and loved him to show him he was worthy to be loved. You know Rudy didn't have to confess anything to me if he didn't want to. I feel like God convicted him so much he couldn't take it anymore. In the process of all the lies, he literally didn't know who he was anymore, and it scared him.

Then suddenly, the great recession hit in 2008. We started to get phone calls after phone calls canceling the contracts with Rudy. We were really scared, not knowing what to do. I did my first Kiddie Kitchen party in May 2008. I was still taking classes and working at the school P/T and helping a friend of mine with paperwork for her interior design business. Rudy was trying to do work wherever he could even if they paid him very little. At the same time, we were trying to heal and keep our family's head above water.

Then on December 12, 2008, we had a court hearing for an eviction. We did everything we could to avoid this from happening, even sold our car to pay the rent; we went on welfare, applied for food stamps so we could feed the kids, but our fears were made real and we were given till January 7, 2009 to get out or be forcefully put out. We lost everything and became homeless. On January 6, I remember sitting in the living room among all the packed boxes,

167

holding the phone in my hand, not knowing who to call. Suddenly, my aunt calls me and I was so glad she called, then she tells me she called to ask for my sister's phone number. I gave it to her and told her what was happening to us and that I have nowhere to go and I'm homeless. In my heart, I was hoping she would have compassion on me and offer me her living room floor. She says well, these things happen; I'm almost in the same boat, silence…Okay, she says, so talk to you later. I hung up the phone and felt so discouraged and hurt. I called my mother and told her what was happening, and she said, oh okay, yeah, things are tough here too…silence…So, I said okay then mom, love you. She said love you too and hung up. I was praying that one of them would quickly call when they realize they didn't offer my family a place to sleep. I waited for a few minutes in anticipation but nothing. Holy crap! Now what? I felt like I had no family when I needed them the most. I was so scared inside.

The home we were going to purchase—gone, our cars—gone, our kids were looking at us for solutions. Rudy and I had to figure this out and fast. Ernest went to rent a room at his friend's parents' home; Steph was still living with her mom. Justin was back home with us after having a traumatic time at his father's home at the hands of his stepmother who hated him and treated him like garbage.

Our dear friends offered us a short stay in their home. We were embarrassed and devastated but also felt some relief until my friend told me my kids weren't allowed to stay over, only Rudy and me. I remember feeling like someone kicked me in the chest and I felt so much pain in my chest when we had no choice but to send Justin to live with his father again. That caused me so much unrest; I had to explain to Justin that this would be temporary if he can hang in there; he was

168

trying to be such a good boy about it and tell me he will be fine.

Unless someone has been in this situation, it's hard to understand how demeaning this felt for us. Here we are, a full-grown married couple given rules and conditions and we had no choice but to put our tail between our legs and accept the circumstances of our situation. It was sobering sleeping in our friends' cold living room on the floor because they were the only ones that offered. We were so grateful to them for this, but quite a few times, we didn't tell our friends we slept in our car, so we weren't a burden to anyone and felt like we had a little dignity.

We called around everywhere to different services; our friend was trying to get us into a shelter as fast as possible. I'm sure it was a mixture of wanting to be helpful and not wanting to be responsible for a couple living in their home. I can't say that I blame them; unfortunately, the shelters were full all over the state and most of the food pantries had no food. I will never forget when my husband had to go to person to person in Darien to get a bag of food, and he called me, crying hysterically on the phone from the pain, fear, and embarrassment he felt because he blamed himself for us losing everything. We were in a desperate state. We also felt so helpless because there were so many people going through the same thing and there was nothing we could do to help them.

One day, crying out to God, I said, "This is so unfair. You told me to quit my job and go to school, why then is this happening?" Suddenly, I heard God clearly say in my heart, *"I told you to be obedient; I never told you it would be easy."* I said, "You're right God, so I will make you proud and be the best student you've ever seen." So, I was determined and got up early every day, cleaned my friends' living room and

169

was at NCC before they opened so I can be the first one in the doors to do my studies and not distress my friends. I was so happy that we were required to wear uniforms because I didn't have many clothes and had to wear the same things sometimes day after day. So, the uniform helped me a lot.

I prayed, studied, and kept my P/T student job at the school, tried to book as many birthday parties as I could, which wasn't many at all because no one was spending money. My poor husband was trying to find work anywhere he could, doing whatever he could. Even having an income of $400-$500 a month was hard to come by.

During all of these, I kept up with my grades. We kept holding on to God and His word and faithfulness; we kept going to therapy. My friends got a larger home, so we were able to rent a room from them but they had us sign a contract for a few months, so we had to find a place quick so that we can move once again. Justin was getting sick a lot at his father's house and my friend still didn't want him to live with us, so we needed to find a place that would allow me to be with my son. I love my friend, and she had her reasons, but I was extremely hurt that she couldn't understand that my child needed me like her children needed her.

I was super desperate because I knew my son was in bad conditions living with his father and his stepmother, but I kept it to myself because I didn't expect my friend to understand. My cousin invited us over for dinner at her home; we went, and she was in a one bedroom but wanted to rent her room out and make her dining room her bedroom. I snagged the opportunity because I didn't know what else to do. It was so hard to be in a single room in a very small apartment and moving around like vagabonds without our kids and literally having to eat at the school culinary classes because we had to pay rent and we had no extra money at all to have anything extra.

We rented around six months with my friend, and we rented the rest of the time with my cousin. One day, Justin's father dropped off Justin to visit for the weekend and he never came back for him. I didn't know what to do; I was so scared but I told my cousin Maria what happened and she allowed Justin to live with us, and we built him a bed over ours. When Stephanie came over to visit, she was so small, so we set up some cushions on plastic crates next to our bed and made her a little bed that she thought was cool. We were homeless until April 2010. One year and four months. In my opinion, this is longer than anyone should have to be without their family together and a place to call home. I don't know how in the world we did it but by the grace of God.

When we finally rented a small apartment in Norwalk, I was in the store with Justin and Ernest, and we were buying things for back-to-school, and Justin was supposed to go to live with his dad again because his father wanted him to finish the school year there. I didn't want Justin to go, but I thought maybe he should so he can finish what he started because Justin was always moving back and forth as he pleased and that was not good for him.

As we were shopping in Walmart, Justin started crying in the store. I asked him what was wrong, and he said, *mommy, please don't send me back to my dad's, please.* I asked why. He tells me that his stepmother makes him wait outside all night after school until his dad comes home around 9 pm and sometimes later than that because she doesn't want him in the house when his father isn't there. My heart sank to the floor. He says, mom, she only feeds me flour and water mixed in a bowl and calls it porridge while her kids get to eat cereal or whatever food she makes them. I

171

couldn't believe what he was telling me. No wonder he was sick all the time and had bad stomach problems. I just grabbed him and started crying with him in the middle of the aisle; *sweetheart, why have you waited so long to tell me this*? My poor baby was holding all this in because he knew he couldn't live with me while I was at my friend's home and he didn't want to cause me any more problems. I knew that every time I picked him up, his clothes smelled really bad, like wet moldy laundry but I thought it was because he didn't want to wash his clothes, but it was because she kept his clothes in the basement on the wet, damp floor and made him get dressed downstairs in the basement. *Holy shit, if I see this bitch, I'm going to kill her.* There was no way in hell I was going to let my baby keep suffering at the hands of this witch. I called my son's father and ripped him a new one. I forewarned him that if I see his little wife, I was going to clean up the streets of Norwalk with her face. He couldn't believe what I was saying, so I made my son tell him the truth. This happened almost a decade ago and I can still feel the pain as if it just happened.

Now that my son was home, I had to focus. I had to remain strong; I needed to finish school so I can help take care of my family and now that we had a place to call home, it felt like we were back on some steady ground.

I knew in my heart that I couldn't move forward without also talking to my dear friend. Their family was the only one besides my cousin that opened the door to Rudy and me when we had no one, and I didn't want to keep this offense in my heart about my child not living with me and me secretly feeling like we were an inconvenience to them. I just knew that she meant too much to me to let this build up and destroy something that means so much to me.

172

So, I prayed for God to give me the right words and the courage to speak with her. I took a deep breath, and I dialed her number. She picked up right away and we started talking about my new little apartment and how nice it felt to have something to call ours again no matter how small it was. Then I said, *sis, we need to talk about something that has hurt me and has been bothering me for a while now.* She said okay. I continued, *you mean the world to me and I want you to know that when we went homeless, I completely was humbled and grateful when you offered us your home. However, I must tell you that you hurt me deeply when you didn't let my children come with us. It was shameful and hurtful enough to lose all we had, but then to be given the condition of not having my kids and looking for them to be elsewhere was salt on an open wound. I felt like you thought my kids weren't any good and yours shouldn't be around them; I have been struggling with whether or not to bring this up to you, but I love you too much to let this fester in my heart. I want to resolve how I feel so it doesn't take away this sisterhood we have.*

My amazing dear friend started crying on the phone and she said, *I am so sorry Neena, I don't know why I did that but I regret how I handled that whole situation. I realized recently in prayer that I have a really hard time trusting people and making sure no one will take advantage of me. Please, forgive me.*

I started crying as well, and we both just loved each other and all ill feelings were completely gone. We are closer than sisters today! Even today, when I bring it up to joke about it, she looks at me and tells me to stop; she doesn't want to be reminded. I just love her!! I am eternally grateful for who she is and the fact that she heard me and my heart and didn't become angry or judge me!

173

I was so happy to get that over with. Then I feel like God is saying, I still have more people to forgive, and He brings my monster to my thoughts. NO WAY! He doesn't deserve my forgiveness. I didn't do anything to him; I was little and he hurt me most of my life. By the way, God, why isn't he dead yet?

I feel God say; *you need to forgive him to be set free.* Uh-uh, no way, Lord, that man should be begging for my forgiveness. I should be okay with not forgiving him. He has no liver left from all his alcoholism and is still alive and kicking; I don't get it. My life was really hard and he has a lot to do with it. I just want him to die already so that I don't have to deal with it. I feel God say, do not be like Jonah, do what I am asking you to do so you can be set free.
FINE! I'll see him, but I don't like this, and I'm pissed off about it. I call my brother and say, *hi, brother, are you by any chance seeing your father any time soon*? Of course, he says *yes, actually we are going to see him next weekend, why, do you want to come*? I said *yes, God is making me.* My brother, who knew what his father did to me says, *okay, are you sure*? I said, *yes, believe me, this is not my idea*! My brother was a little skeptical; I can't say that I blame him, so he called me the following weekend to make sure I still wanted to go. The truth is, I didn't want to go. I wasn't sure how I was going to react just seeing this man again after so many years. What was I going to say to him? Would he even admit to anything he ever did to me? Can I hold myself back from punching him in the face several times? I wasn't sure how this was going to go down. I looked to my husband and said, *Rudy, please pray for me; I'm not sure if I can handle this, but I don't want you to go; I need to do this on my own.*

The weekend arrived and my brother, his wife and family, picked me up and off we went to New York to see his father. The closer we get to his address, the more I feel like vomiting. We get there, and his father happens to be outside because he was expecting us. I'm walking towards him and I feel like I'm about to faint, and become nervous and lightheaded and nauseous. The monster looks at me. *Oh, my goodness, my beautiful daughter, I can't believe you're here. I've missed you; I haven't seen you in years, how are you*? All I kept thinking is, *is this guy for real*? Then, some friends of his walks by and he introduces me as his beautiful daughter. I wasn't sure what to say; I just shook their hands and nodded my head. Nice to meet you.

      I look at my brother and his wife and ask them to please leave me alone with him for a few moments. My brother looks at me suspiciously and says, *are you sure you want us to leave you alone with him*? I wonder if my brother thought I was going to beat his father down in the middle of the street. I said yes, I need to do this, and I need to do this by myself. So, when my brother and his wife and kid were walking away, I went up to my father and said, *you and I need to talk*. He said, *I know we do*. I said, *you have done some evil things to me, things that no one should do to a kid. I wonder if you even remember half of the things you did because you were always so drunk you probably don't even know all of the abuse. Because of you and everything you've done to me, I have made bad decisions, and my life has been hard. I hated you for everything you have done to me. And you probably don't even remember what you've done*. He looks at me and says, *I remember everything I've done to you and I hate myself for what I did*.

      I couldn't believe he admitted it. I got really close to him, eye to eye, nose to nose, looked at him and with my teeth clenching together, said, *I choose to forgive you; I choose to forgive you! The only reason I am here is because*

175

God wants me to forgive you. I choose to forgive you; you will no longer have power over me! I take back everything you've taken from me. My eyes started tearing up, and he used his hands to wipe away my tears and said, I understand. And he grabbed and hugged me, and I hugged him back and, in that instant, all of my anger, rage, shame, bitterness, hate, fear, broke in the spirit. I literally felt a shift in my life that very moment. I knew God released me from the prison of what this man did to me. I looked at him and said, *God must love you because I literally wanted you to die before I came here today.* He said, *there's no way God loves me, after all I have done.* I said, *on the contrary, He really does love you because I would not be standing here today if it weren't for Him. You are forgiven! Now, go and pray and ask God to forgive you and come into your life.* At this moment, my brother and his family walked up. My brother looked at me and asked, *is everything okay?* I said, *yes, absolutely okay; I am free and I never have to deal with this again or see him again.* This is done. I kissed my ex-stepfather on the cheek and asked him to make sure he prays, and it was done.

God, thank you for setting me free; now it was time to really buckle down and focus. I must get my degree and show my kids that no matter how hard things get or what people do to you, you can overcome with God on your side.

Justin was struggling with school and always getting into some sort of trouble. I was in school and working a lot, so I had to try and balance all of this and still take care of his needs. I wanted to quit so many times, but Rudy wouldn't let me. He would say there is no way we went through all of this so you can quit, you will finish what God has told you to do.

Justin was having a hard time adjusting to all the changes in his life with the back and forth from us to his dad's home. He started showing it by rebelling against our house rules. He was struggling and experimenting with marijuana, ecstasy and other drugs. We found packaged marijuana bags in his school backpack, and he started hanging out with horrible, dangerous, bad groups of people. I would constantly be praying that God would intervene and help me with my son. I needed to save his life. But how? What can I do? I needed to hurry up and finish school so I can concentrate even more on my son and have the finances I need to take care of him somehow. I was trying to have him finish school; I would ground him and not let him go out so he couldn't associate with these people and do drugs. I didn't want to lose my son to the streets. I started him with a therapist to help him deal with his anger issues and to see if there was anything we can do to help him overcome his brokenness. Unfortunately, Justin is a lot like me and is very hardheaded; he got deeper into using drugs every day and associating with people I knew would bring him to destruction.

Therapy seemed to work a bit, and he seemed to get some balance. I tried my hardest to rule with an iron fist so he could fear the consequences of his actions. All the while, trying to keep myself focused on what God was doing in my life.

Boy, God is so very faithful and fair; I got every scholarship I ever applied for through my time at NCC. I got my culinary certificate and then kept going to get my associates degree. I graduated with a 4.0 GPA; I was the valedictorian for the class of 2011. I was in the papers, radio, T.V, and magazines around the country as an inspirational story. Justin and Ernest went to my graduation and saw that all the hard work was for something great.

I have zero ideas on how God gave me the strength to do all of this and how I did what I did. I was happy to have

177

my husband by my side, not letting me quit every time I wanted to give up; my kids being so supportive even though it was hard for them, especially Justin who needed me and my love the most because of what he was working through. I just had to make them and God proud and show them and God that I will trust Him even in the midst of what looks impossible. And He showed me; He was trustworthy.

I then asked Him, "Dad, can I continue my education and get my bachelor's degree?" I will be the first one in my family to get a bachelor's degree! I almost immediately got a letter from Monroe in NY telling me they wanted to offer me a scholarship because they read my story.

In the middle of these joyful things, Justin started to get worse. He was always out when we were at school and work. He was coming home with black eyes and bruises and constantly telling me he fell on his skateboard or in the school somewhere. I knew he was lying and he was probably getting in trouble, but I couldn't prove it. Then the school calls me to tell me he was carrying weed in school and he got suspended. Then he was running the streets with people who didn't care about him, and when we kept finding weed in our home even after we warned him several times, I couldn't take it anymore; so, I kicked him out.

He went to live with his girlfriend, and when he started doing crazy stuff over there, she kicked him out too, so now he was in the streets and sleeping over friends' homes. I cried every night, wondering where he was and what he was doing. Was he eating? Was he sleeping outside? Was he going to be found overdosed? Jesus, please help me, please hear my cry. This was the most painful experience I've ever had. Then about six weeks later, he comes to my home, and he was skin and bones. I almost fainted when I saw him because my baby looked like a crackhead and he

178

was so bruised up, and his clothes were dirty. I had to hold on to the bed while he was standing in my bedroom so he couldn't tell I felt faint. He said, "Mom, I need to come back home. I have nowhere at all to stay. The place where I was staying is no longer safe. I thought they were my friends but when I woke up today, they were all wearing my clothes and playing my video game system and took my camera and when I told them to take off my things, they all jumped me, beat me up pretty bad and stole all my things, then kicked me out of the house while laughing at me."

I said, *but you chose your friends over being in this house where we took care of you, remember? We gave you simple rules, and you decided that your friends were more important than following my rules. You even quit school in your last year of high school. I didn't raise you this way, J.* He says, *mom, I'm so sorry, please let me stay; I have nowhere to go. I don't want to go out there.*
I looked at my baby and said, *I'm sorry Justin, I know it's Wednesday but I have a class, and I will have some time from 1 pm to 2 pm on Friday*; *we will talk about it then.* He looked at me in disbelief, and said, *mom, you're not hearing me. I can't go back out there; I have nowhere at all to go; I will have to sleep in the streets until Friday. Oh, and by the way*, I said, *you owe me $200 for the rent when you left. Bring me the $200 you owe me and we will discuss it then.* He replied, *mom, I don't have that kind of money, my friends stole everything from me.* I said, *well, you still have a cell phone, so figure it out.* He turned around with his head down, and I walked him out the door. *Don't forget I will only be available between 1 and 2 pm*, I said. I came back inside and fell to the floor bawling in pain. I have never felt this much pain in my chest since my grandparents died. This was the worst feeling in my life; it felt like losing a child. I didn't know if I just

179

sentenced my son to death. I prayed and prayed for angels to surround him and keep him safe everywhere he went.

When Friday came, he showed up at 1 pm, handed me the $200 and told me how he now had no phone because he sold it to get me the money he owed me. We sat and talked about the rules and how if he broke them again, he was out permanently; no more chances.

I have to admit; I was a very happy mother having him back in the house where I knew he was safe. I was so disappointed in him for not finishing school and making the life choices he was making. I raised him better than that, and I couldn't understand how or why he would choose these things. It wasn't very long before he was back at it, in the streets with horrible characters he called friends, and I just couldn't take it anymore. I asked God for an answer to save my son. Suddenly, his ex-stepmother, the one I wanted to 'kill,' calls me up and says she wants to take Justin with her out of state. She says she heard all that Justin is going through and wants to make up with him and she desires an opportunity to help him through the crisis. I couldn't believe my ears. Could this be the answer? So, I brought him a one-way ticket to Florida and sent him to an unknown place. This needed to be as dramatic and fast as it could be before his friends convince him to stay. I brought the ticket, sent him to his father's house for a couple of days and off to the airport with a few bucks and a bookbag full of clothes. I will do whatever I have to do to save my children. When I was praying about this dramatic move, I got a scripture from God for Justin; *Jeremiah 29:13-14 You will seek me and find me when you seek me with all your heart. I will be found by you," declares the Lord, "and will bring you back from captivity. I will gather you from all the nations and places <u>where I have banished you</u>," declares the Lord, "and will*

180

bring you back to the place from which I carried you into exile."

Even though his ex-stepmother said all of that, true to her nature, it wasn't long until she mistreated Justin again and put him out in the streets, he found a friend out there and rented a room with them and even when times became tough and unbearable, I didn't allow him to come back home and quit. He was going to see this through and make his own way. I refused to lose my child to drugs and the streets. God is so good!

While all of these was going on, I kept my head in the books. Driving back and forth to Monroe for school, working in the college, doing parties on weekends and catering on the side.

Wow, believe it or not, God, being the faithful God that He is, paid for my culinary certification, associate's degree and bachelor's degree in full. How, you ask? Every time I asked God for money to pay for it, I would apply for a different scholarship and would get a check in the mail every time.

I didn't sit back and expect Him to do it all; I put in my part of the work. I worked several jobs at a time; I started my own small business. I worked as a personal chef; I worked at restaurants; I wanted to show God how grateful I am and was doing it because He did it for me; God is so fair. Even though this journey with school was hard and took me longer to accomplish than most people because I had to work different jobs and overcome lots of obstacles, I'm glad I went through it, it was to give me strength and skills I needed to be successful. I currently have my dream job as an Executive Chef and Manager of an amazing place that serves local, fresh and creative dishes. God blessed me to be able to start this kitchen from scratch because it was newly built. Because I was obedient and faithful, God blessed me abundantly.

Rudy and I got stronger and stronger in our relationship, even though it seemed like everything around us was crumbling at times. I was getting to know him for real this time, and I liked him. He is a really great guy. He was getting to know himself, and now, he is no longer afraid of being who he is, and he is authentic, full of integrity, strong, loving, dependable, and now, sometimes, is too blunt and honest. I guess I shouldn't complain about that; I know I'm never getting lied to again. The pain of this experience is beyond a lesson learned. He has developed a really strong and meaningful relationship with God; now I see why God said I am making him new for you. God is so fair. Even when life is hard hitting and feels like you are always on the wrong side of the hit, God will provide you with what you need to overcome a hard-hitting life.

My mother and I are healed and love each other very much. I helped my mom develop a relationship with Jesus, and that has brought so much peace and love to our relationship.

Ernest is doing really well, and I am so proud of the man he has become, responsible, loving, honest, and full of faith. Just a few months ago he called and said, *mom, if it wasn't for you I wouldn't have a connection to God, you are my only connection to God.* I couldn't believe my ears, it was a confirmation that over ten years ago, while I was in the car, I did hear God when He said those exact same words to me.

Justin has found himself, he's off of drugs and is being awakened to everything God has purposed for him. I have cried and prayed so many nights for God to intervene, prayer changes things and I'm excited to see what God is going to do through him.

182

Chris is back in our lives; I have prayed for so many years to hold our son again, praise God! We picked up where we left off and he is really a good young man, smart, articulate and finding his God-given path in life. GOD IS SO FAIR!

Stephanie is our princess and is such a beautiful, young lady, in college and looking forward to growing one day in her career as a video game designer. My one and only daughter, my gift from God.

My aunts and I have also grown and healed in our relationships with each other. My cousin, Maria, is still my special sister in my life.

I still have a relationship with my brothers and sisters from my dad's side. I don't know them all but there are about thirteen of us from what I'm told. I guess my mother wasn't the only women my father wooed.

I cried a lot of tears; there have been a lot of fights, a lot of hard hits, a lot of changes, a lot of discouragements but God has changed my life and the life of my family. He came in and transformed us through the struggles and has made us into who we are today. I'm sure there is more to come. I have definitely been hit hard in life but I am not broken. I have learned to take some hits and give some hits but I will stand. My faith and prayer life has helped me overcome and win these battles. I'm sure I have a lot more battles to come in life, but with God, I can do all things. I can write and talk about all these things in my life because I am FREE.

My Anchor scripture for our family:
Jeremiah 29:11
[11] For I know the plans I have for you," declares the Lord, "plans to prosper you and not to harm you, plans to give you hope and a future.

About the Author

Born and raised in Stamford CT, Neena has a wonderful blended family that includes four beautiful children of three boys and a girl. Having a rough childhood and encountering many challenges has made her the woman she is today—determined, strong, and full of faith in God.

Not really having guidance and a relationship with God until adulthood, she had her first child at the early age of 15 and another one at 21. Neena had to wait in life to go to college. She worked as a medical assistant and ultrasound technician for 15 years, to care for her family.

Moving in faith, she is finally following her childhood passion of being a chef. Neena has a Bachelor's in Hospitality Management and Culinary Management, has two businesses—The Kiddie Kitchen, which is home cooking parties and cooking camps for kids, and The Kitchen After Hours—adult cooking parties, catered events, and cakes. She is now an executive chef and manager and loves that God transformed her path in life.

God is now moving Neena's life in a powerful way. Alongside feeding people physically, He is leading her to feed people spiritually as well, leading Bible studies, inspirational blogs, podcasts, motivational speaking, teachings and becoming an author. Neena's calling is to encourage, support, love and lead people to be the best selves in God they could be.

After so many years of challenges, she finally feels like she's walking in the path and calling that God has written for her.

Thank you from the bottom of my heart for reading my book!! I am going to release another book to share with you all the transformative stories and lessons I have learned from God. I have been through a lot and I know there will be more to come, as I'm sure you have, are, and will be also. I hope this book gives you some hope that although things are hard and seem impossible, nothing is impossible for God.

I really appreciate you! I would love to hear your feedback and what you have to say!!
Let me know if you feel led to share.
God bless you in your quest to have peace, love, and understanding of your calling.

Looking forward to what will encourage, uplift, and help me develop as an author, blog writer, motivational speaker, and encourager.

Blog:
straighttalknosugaradded.com

Podcast on iTunes, Spotify, Sound Cloud:
Straight Talk No Sugar Added

Email:
hello@straighttalknosugaradded.com

Facebook:
https://www.facebook.com/straighttalknosugaradded/

95540138R00111

Made in the USA
Middletown, DE
26 October 2018